semplicità ~ simplicité ~ simplicidad

Dedication

This book is in publication because of my husband's belief in me. He urged me to publish this book because he knows how much I enjoy creating, using & sharing my Page Patterns with others. I also have to thank my son's girlfriend for pushing me to publish this book while we were in the waiting room of the hospital during his shoulder surgery.

Thank You and I Love You

Copyright 2008 by Cheryl Bradbury. The patterns in this book are intended for use in scrapbooks. This book was printed and bound in the United States of America. All rights reserved. No part of this book may be reproduced in any form or by any means without the permission in writing from the author.

Introduction

Scrapbooking is my passion and anything that will give me simplicity in order to get my pages created and finished is an absolute "must have." Many times I would just sit and stare at my photos experiencing what I called "Layout Block," racking my brain to come up with a layout and before I knew it, my free time was over. One day, I was flipping through my favorite Scrapbooking magazine and there they were, staring me in the face…Sketches, the answers to my "Layout Block." I almost fell out of my chair from the excitement of the endless possibilities these sketches would enable me with. Instantly I felt my days of "Layout Block" were coming to an end now armed with these sketches, which I call "Page Patterns."

My mission now was to create my own personal patterns on my computer, allowing me access to them for my digital pictures. I call them page patterns from my years of sewing experience as they remind me of sewing patterns. My patterns grew and grew and grew and before I knew it, I had hundreds upon hundreds of them organized by the number of photos and was still creating and collecting more. For my scrapbooking friends, I printed out copies them telling them how simple and fun these patterns made it to finish a layout. The patterns saved so much time and did away with "Layout Block" and I was actually finishing more pages.

I created "Page Patterns" as the perfect prescription for "Layout Block". It can be turned, flipped, rotated and tweaked to fit your photos just way you need. Incorporated into these patterns are: plain and patterned paper uses and tons of embellishment ideas from brads, buttons, buckles, belts and staples to ribbons, ric-rac, tags, flowers and paperclips for motivation and inspiration in getting your layouts done and caught up.

In the book, I've included an Embellishments Chart, Pattern Size Conversion Charts from the patterns, at their book size, for easy true-size conversion and plenty of empty boxes to add in your own patterns for future layouts.

My hopes are that you enjoy the simplicity of "Page Patterns" as much as I still do.

Just Plain Simplicity
Cheryl Bradbury
Have a Scrappin' 4 Memories Day

Page Patterns

Embellishments Chart

	safety pin		photo corner		
	turn buttons		envelope tie		
	folder tab		frame hangers		
	buckles		charms		
	paper clip		hinge		
	bread tag		staples		
	bookplate		eyelet		
	buttons		ric-rac		
	tags		ribbons		
	metal word plate				
	ribbon tie		swirl clip		
	slide frame		flowers		

4

Page Patterns

Table of Contents

Doubles

2 Photos	9
3 Photos	13
4 Photos	17
5 Photos	23
6 Photos	29
7 Photos	35
8 Photos	41
9 Photos	47
10 Photos	53
11 Photos	59
12 Photos	65
13 Photos	71
14 Photos	75
15 Photos	79
16 Photos	83
17 Photos	87
18 & 19 Photos	91
20 & 21 Photos	95
22 & 23 Photos	99
24 & 25 Photos	103
26 & 27 Photos	107
28 & 29 Photos	111
30 & Up Photos	115

Singles

1 Photo	123
2 Photos	127
3 Photos	131
4 Photos	135
5 Photos	141
6 Photos	147
7 Photos	151
8 & 9 Photos	155
10, 11 & 12 Photos	159

Embellishments Chart 4

Conversion Charts . . . . . 6 & 163

Page Patterns

Patterns Size Conversion Charts

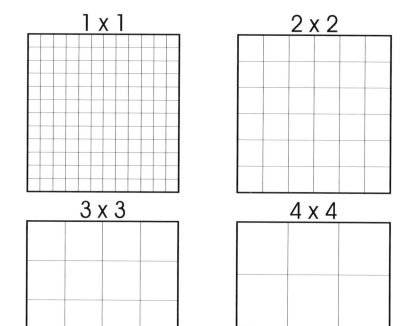

1 x 1
2 x 2
3 x 3
4 x 4

Use these conversion charts in helping to size your photos to fit the pattern your using. When fully sized, these charts and single Page Patterns are 12 x 12 and double Page Patterns are 12 x 24. Easily get correct measurements for your photos or mattings by matching your selected pattern against the conversion chart sizes.

Copy this page on to a Transparency for easier use with the Page Patterns.

Double Page Layout Patterns

Also see my other book:

Totally Toppers & Titles 'The Little Pink Book'
(available at www.amazon.com)

This book is loaded with Titles & Toppers, Quotes, Sayings, Verses, Poems, Prayers, Creeds and more. Also included are some words and sayings translations for a fun impact on your layouts, as well as, hundreds of Title Tips.

There are over 400 Categories to choose from, containing over 10,000 Titles & Toppers, 4,000 Quotes & Sayings, 1,300 Poems, Verses, Prayers, Creeds & over 400 Title Tips.

Double Page Layout Patterns

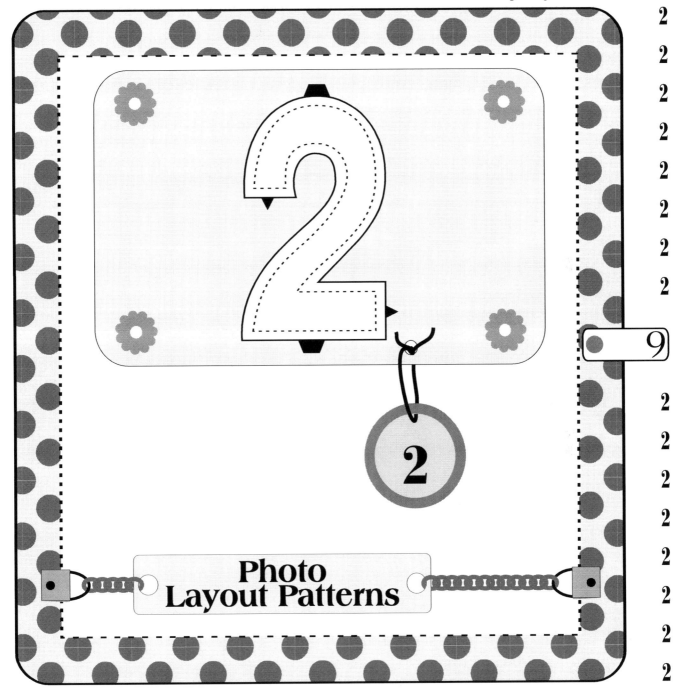

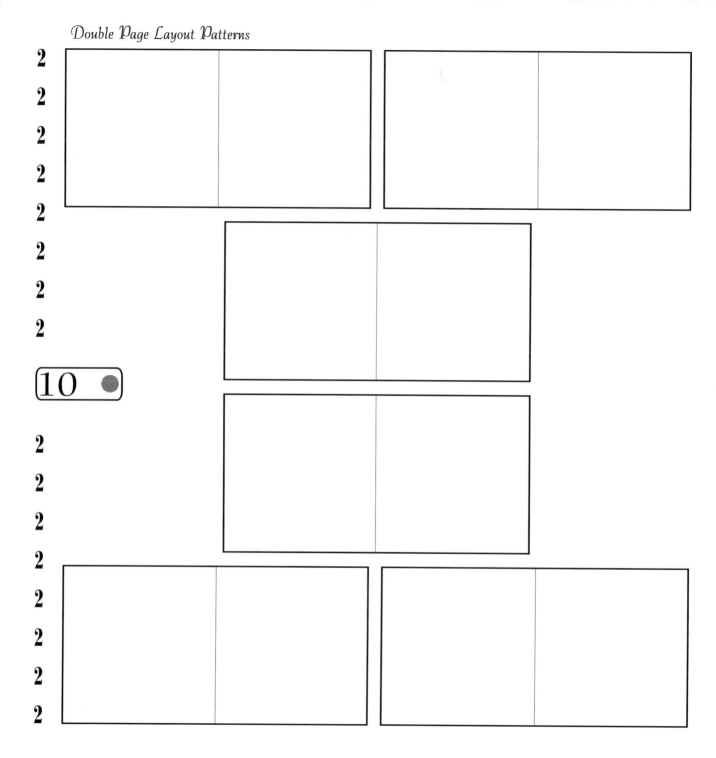

Double Page Layout Patterns

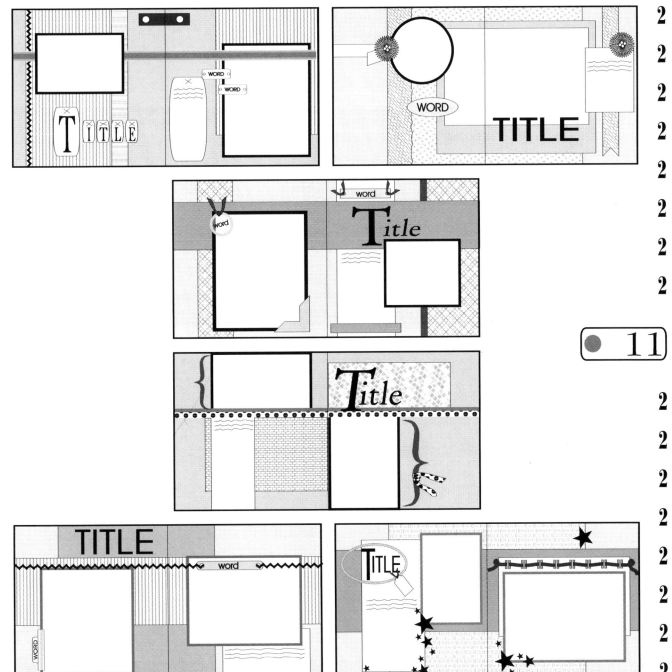

Double Page Layout Patterns

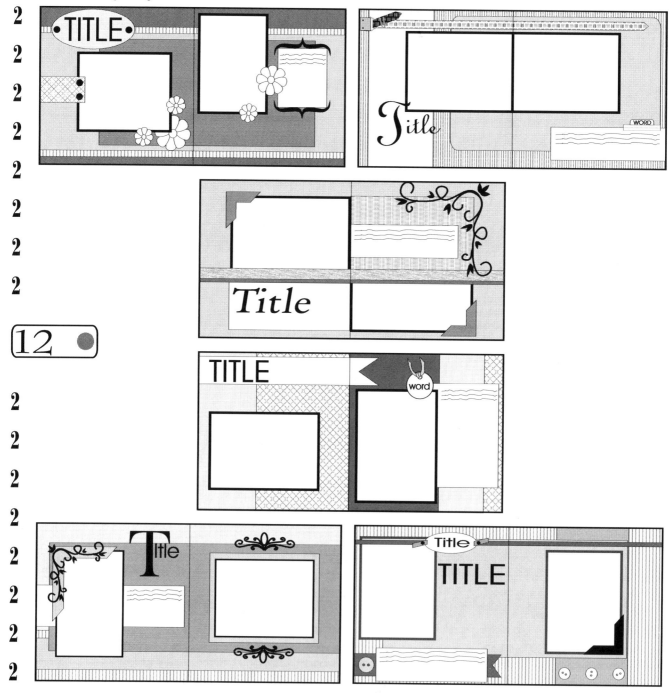

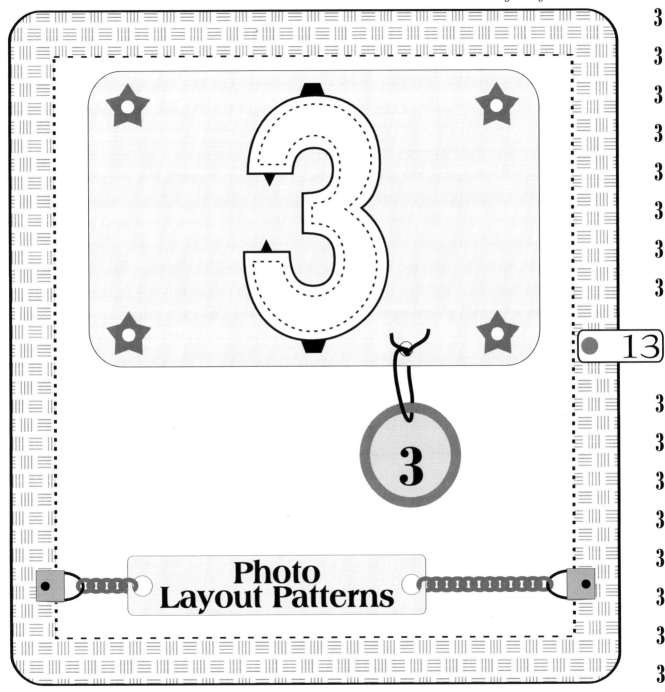

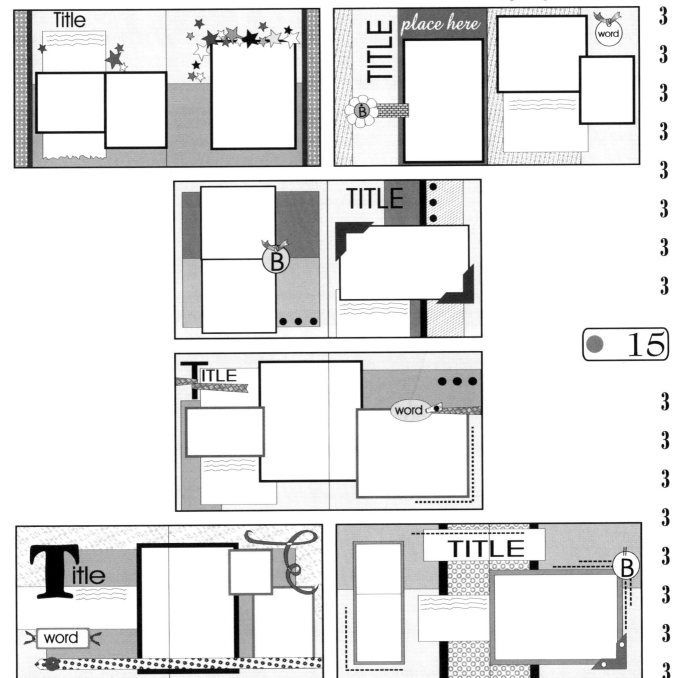

Double Page Layout Patterns

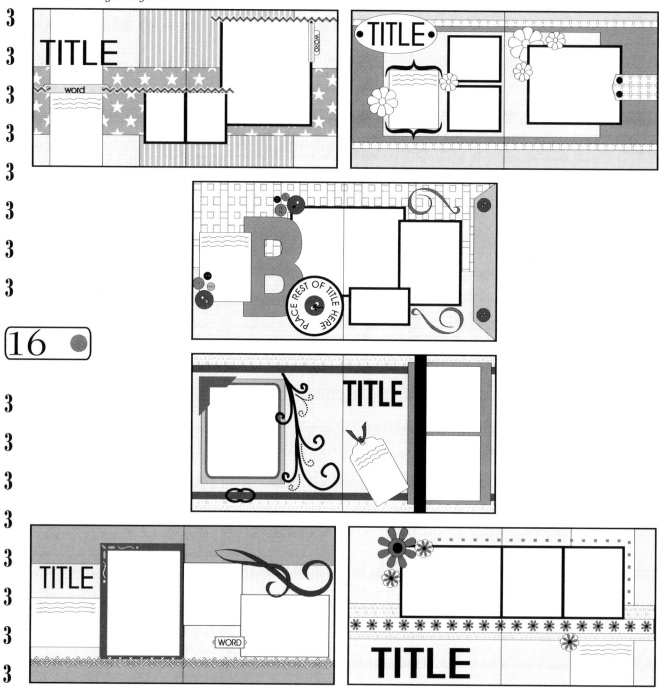

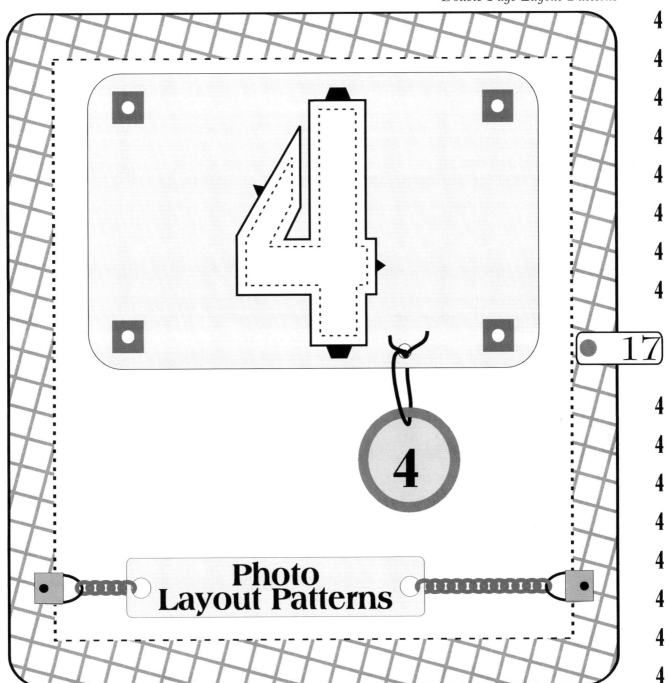

Double Page Layout Patterns

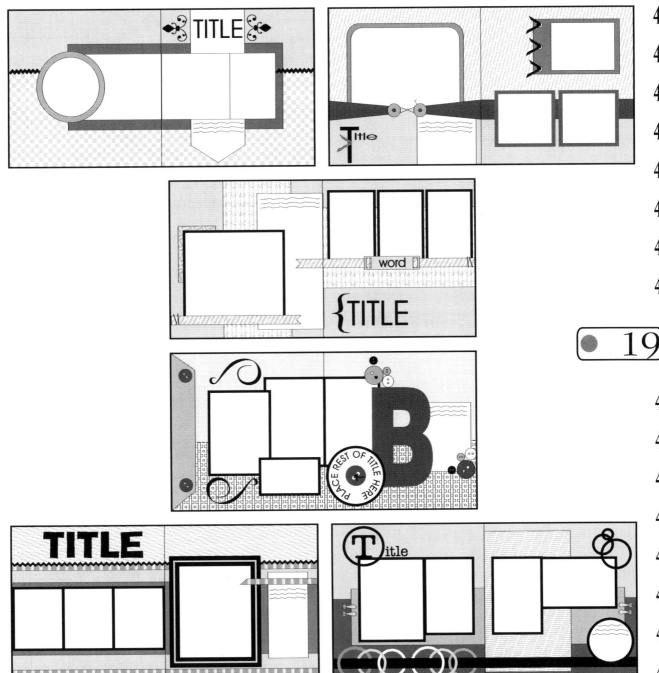

19

Double Page Layout Patterns

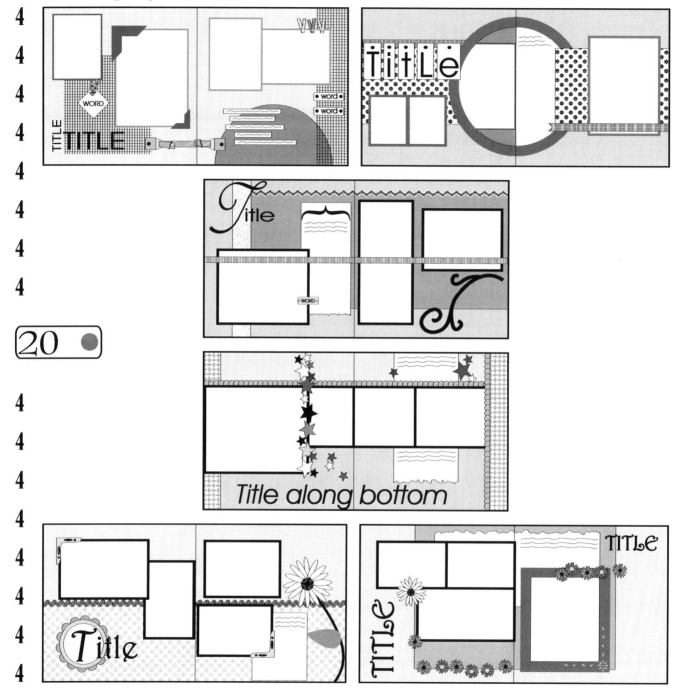

Double Page Layout Patterns

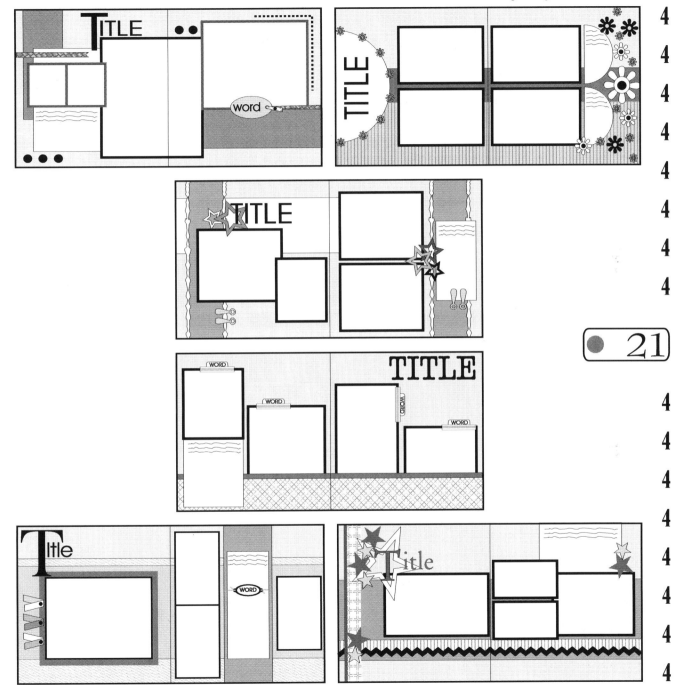

21

Double Page Layout Patterns

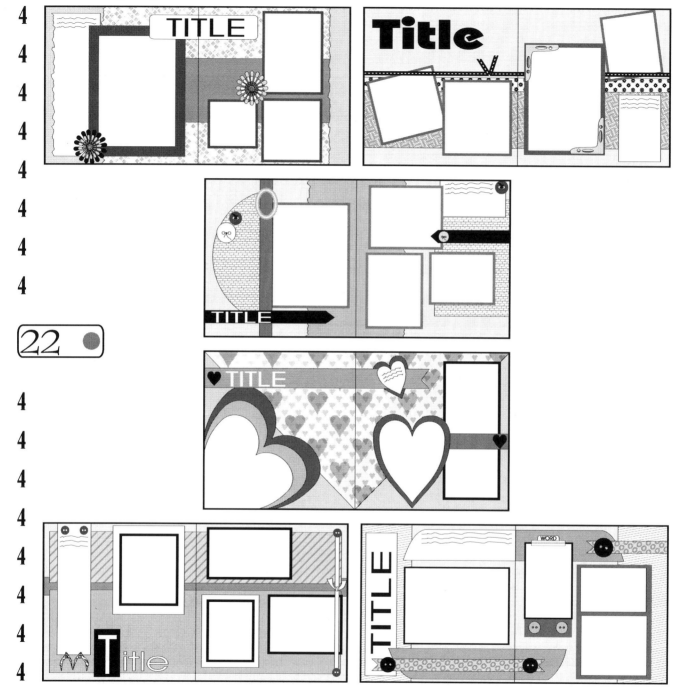

22

Double Page Layout Patterns

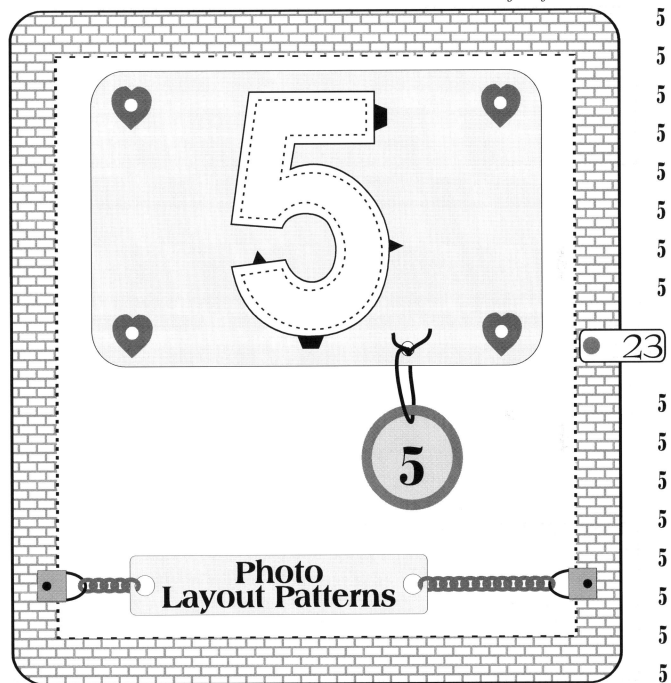

Double Page Layout Patterns

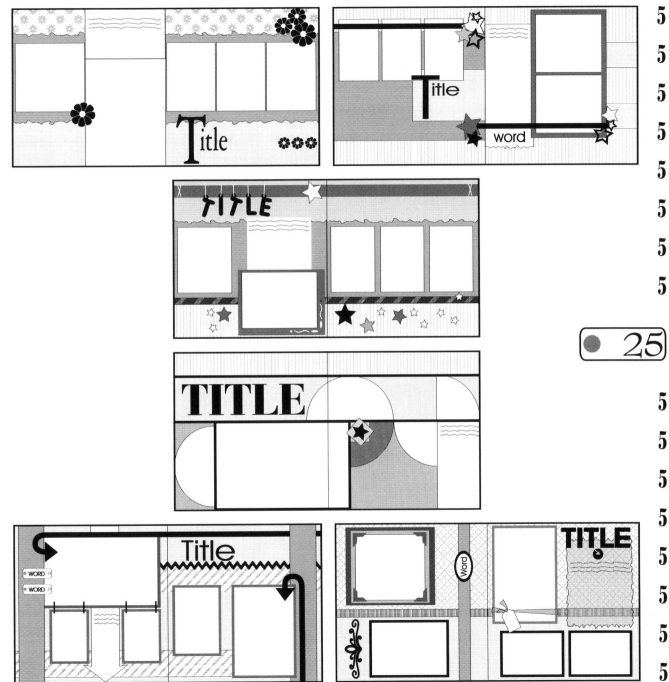

Double Page Layout Patterns

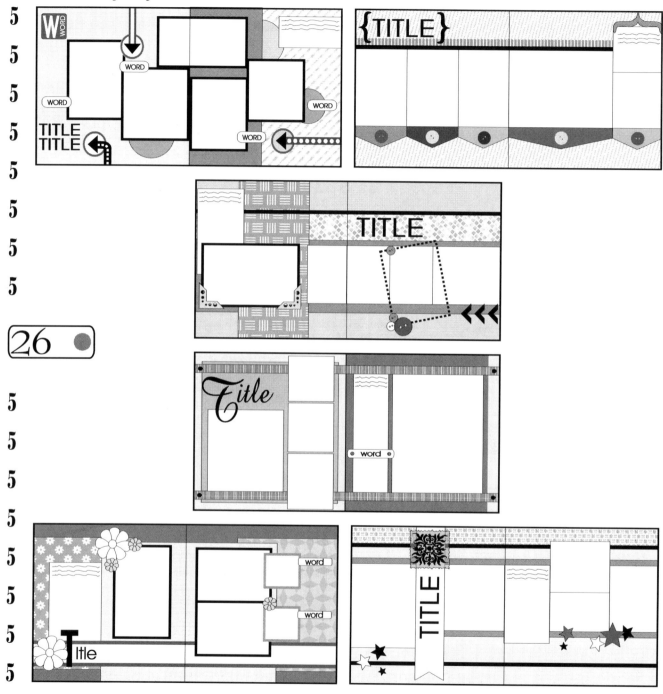

Double Page Layout Patterns

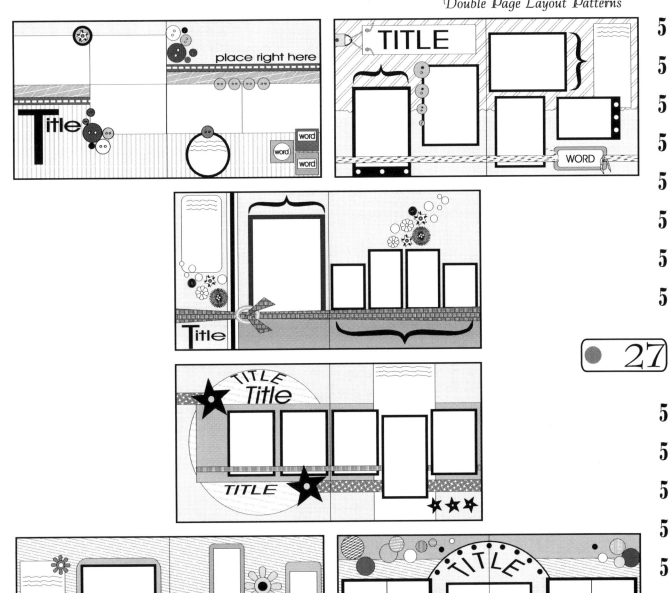

27

Double Page Layout Patterns

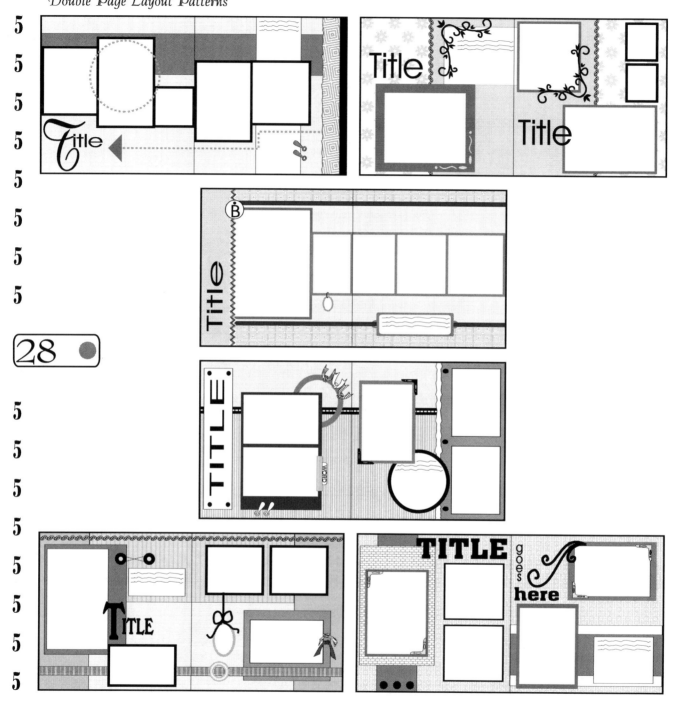

Double Page Layout Patterns

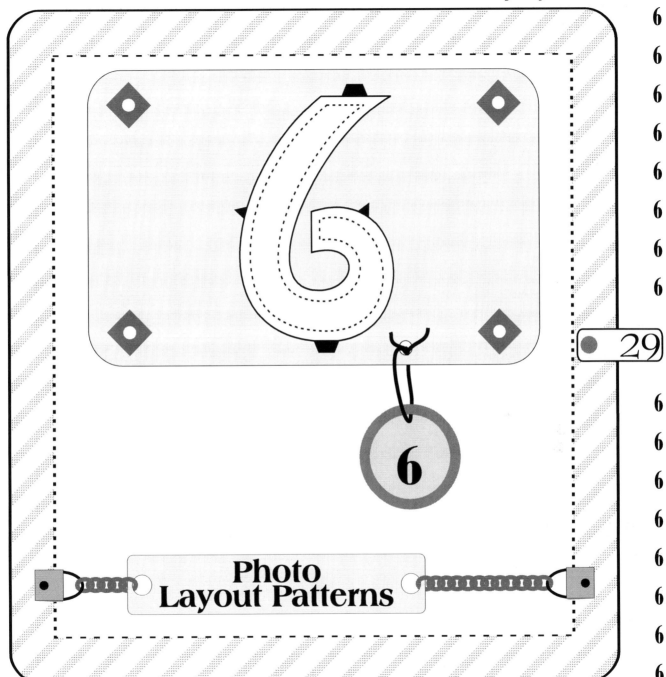

29

Double Page Layout Patterns

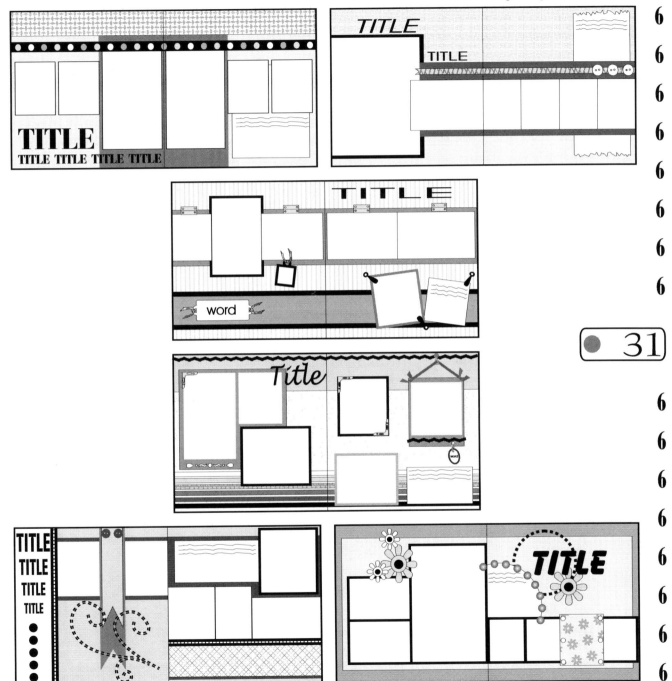

Double Page Layout Patterns

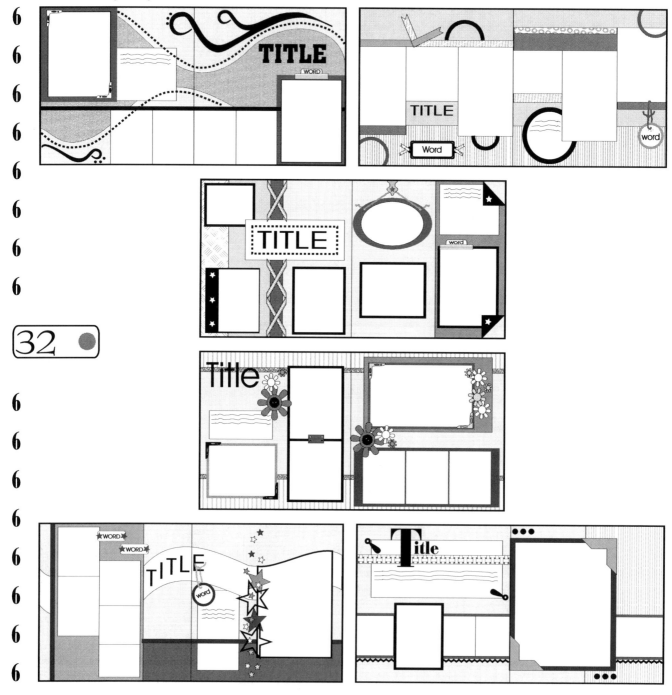

Double Page Layout Patterns

33

Double Page Layout Patterns

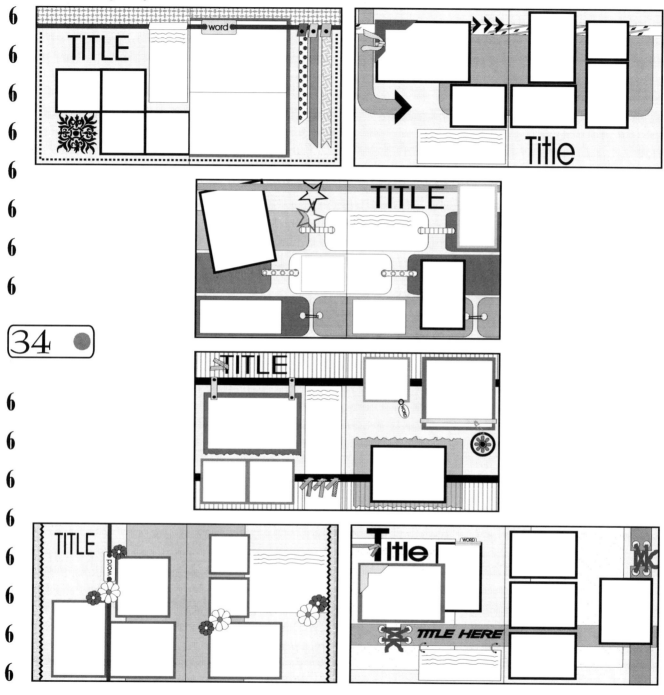

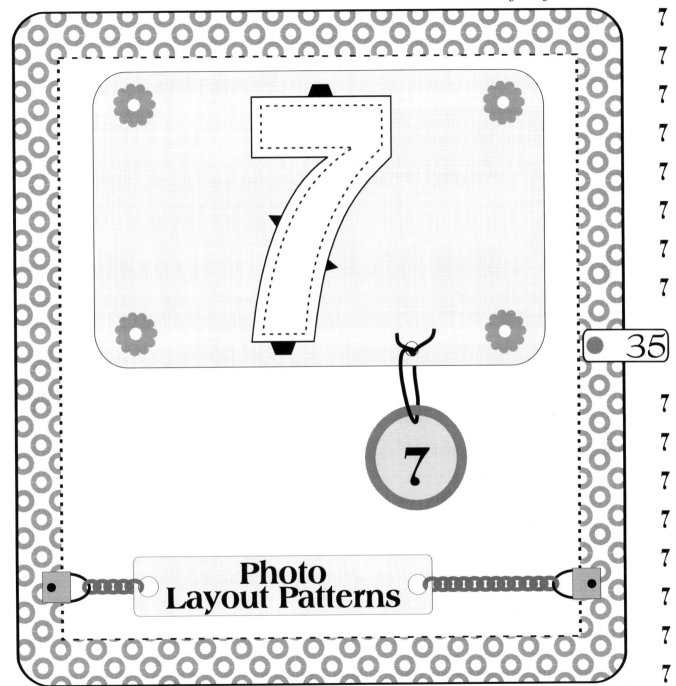

Double Page Layout Patterns

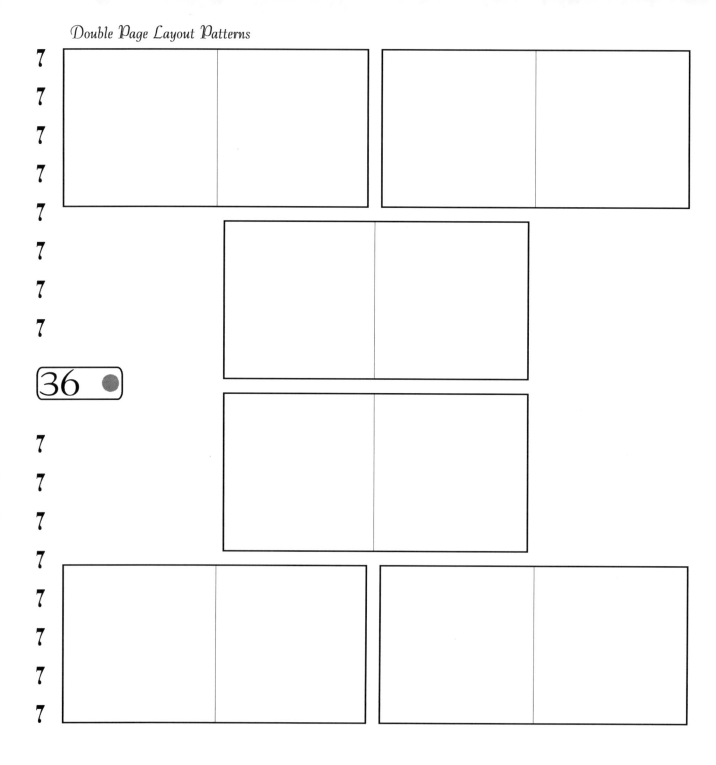

Double Page Layout Patterns

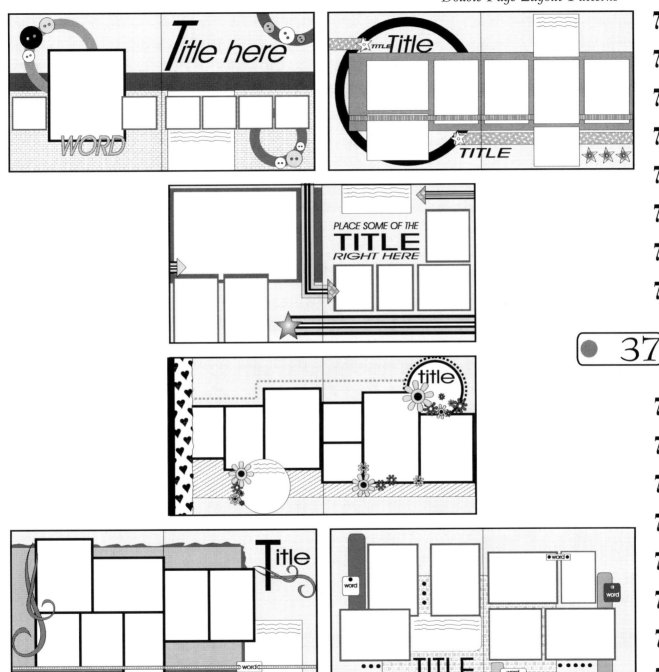

37

Double Page Layout Patterns

Double Page Layout Patterns

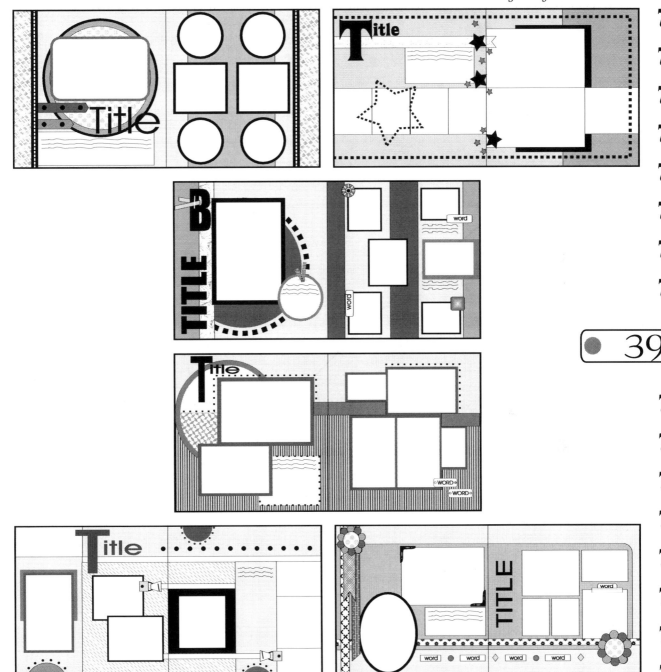

Double Page Layout Patterns

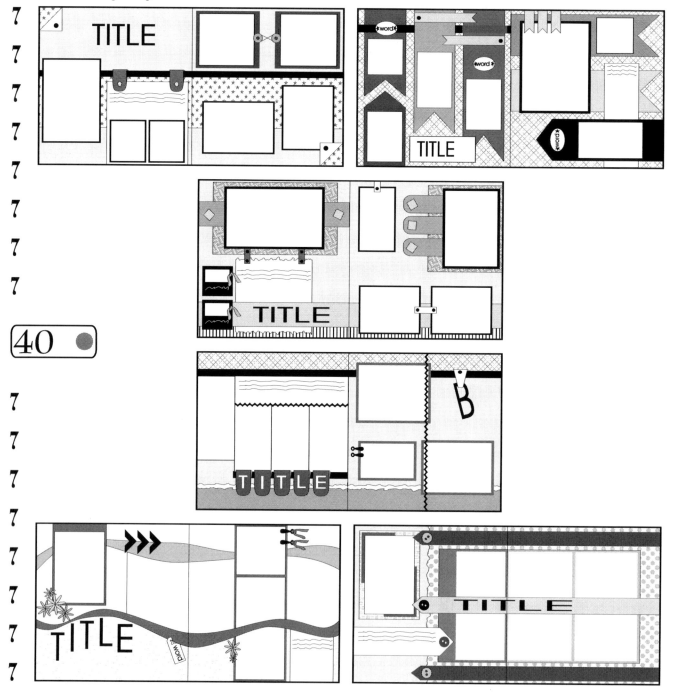

Double Page Layout Patterns

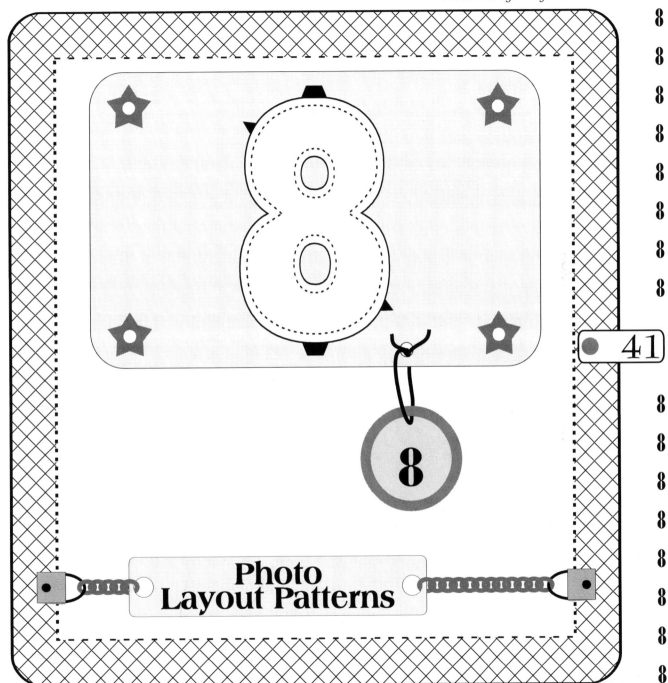

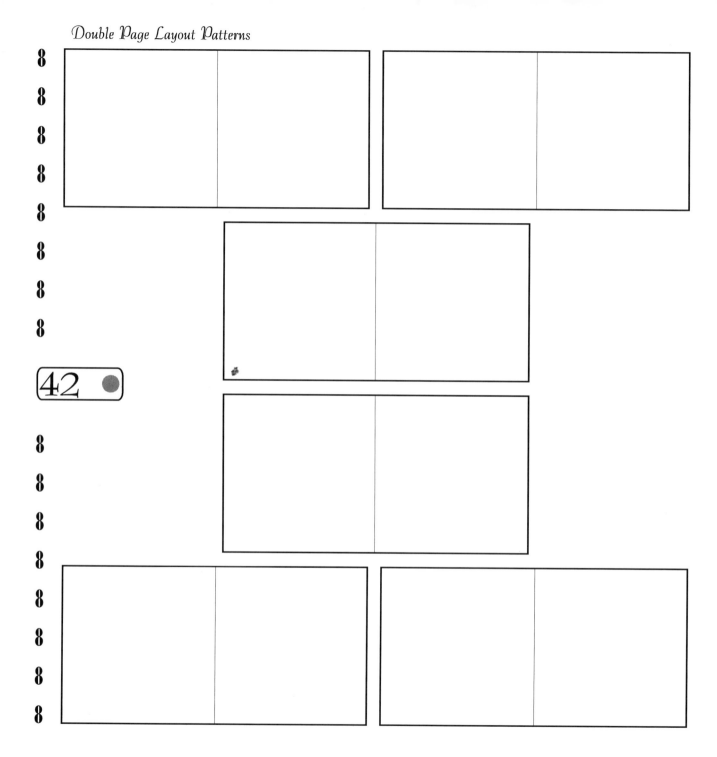

Double Page Layout Patterns

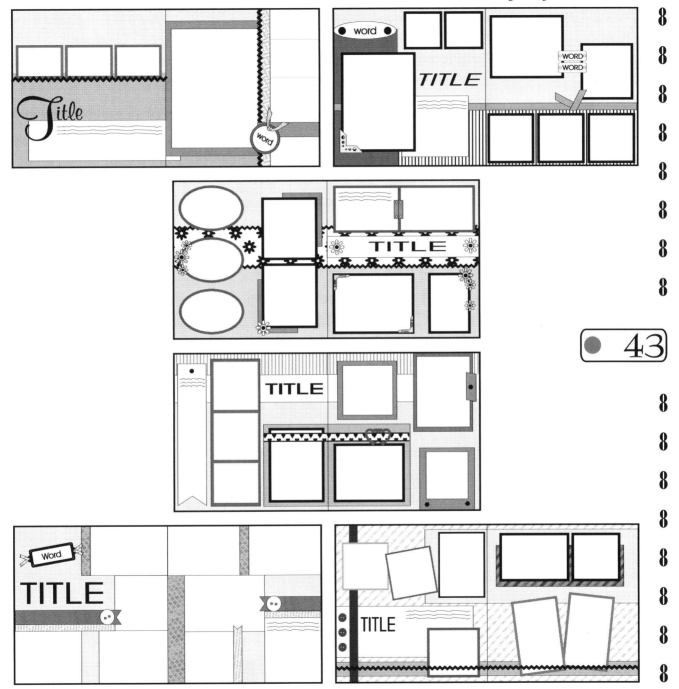

43

Double Page Layout Patterns

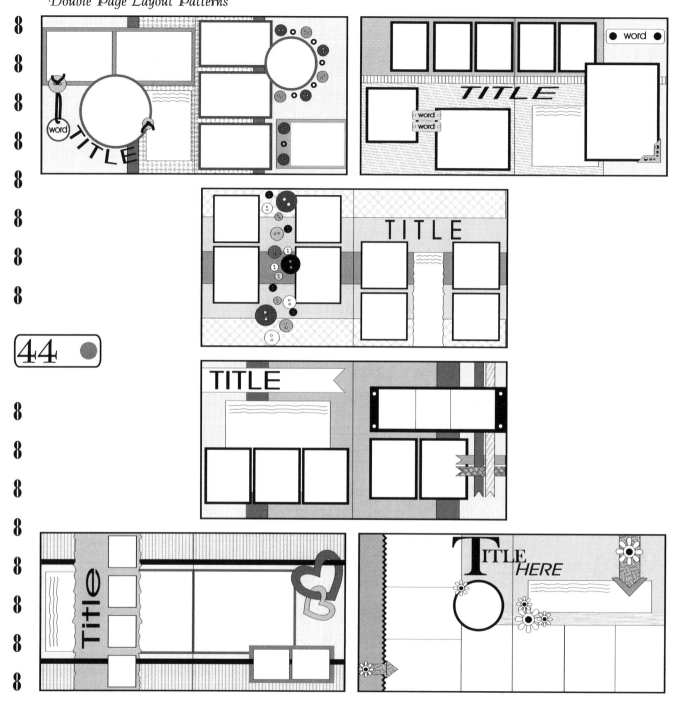

Double Page Layout Patterns

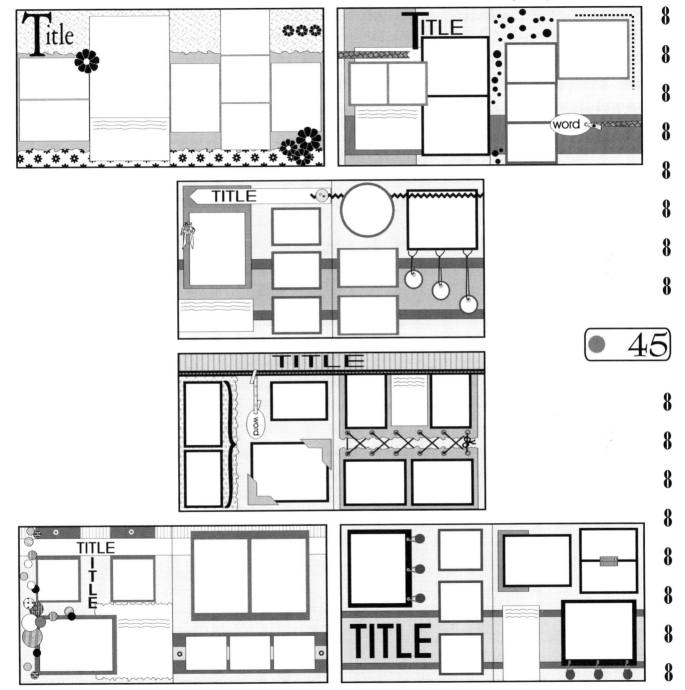

45

Double Page Layout Patterns

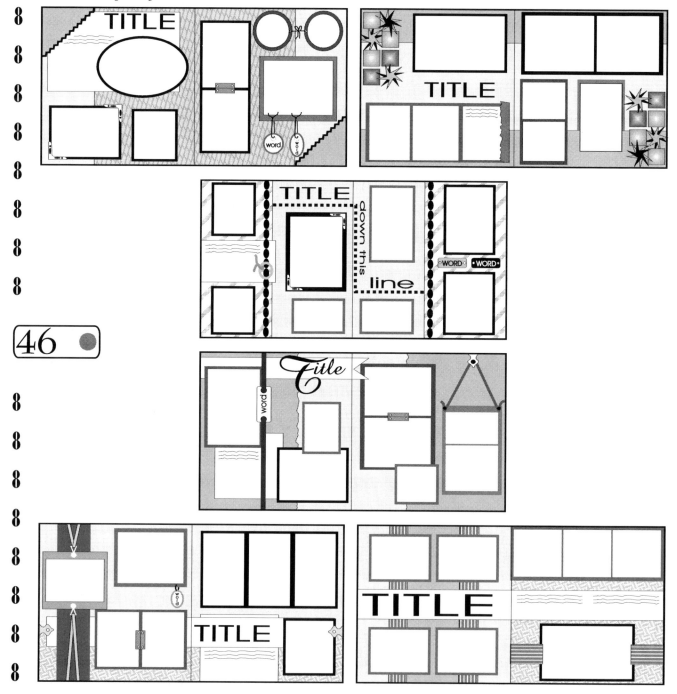

Double Page Layout Patterns

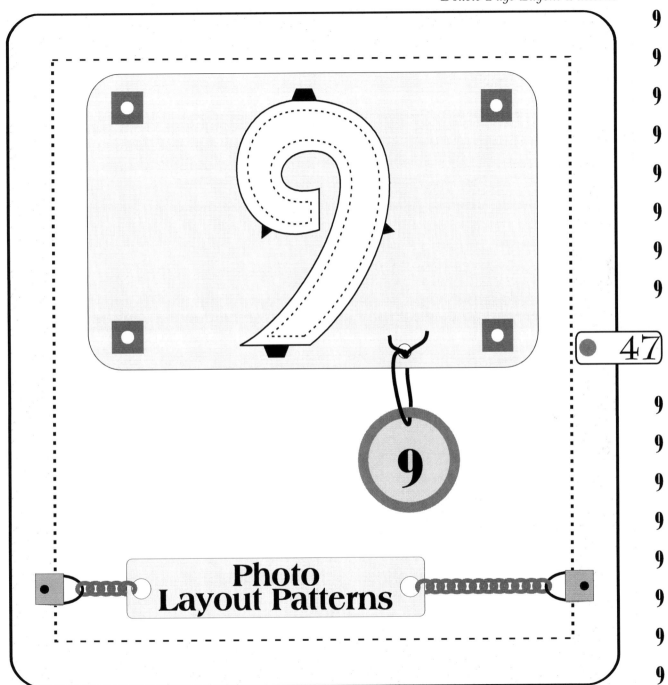

Photo Layout Patterns

47

Double Page Layout Patterns

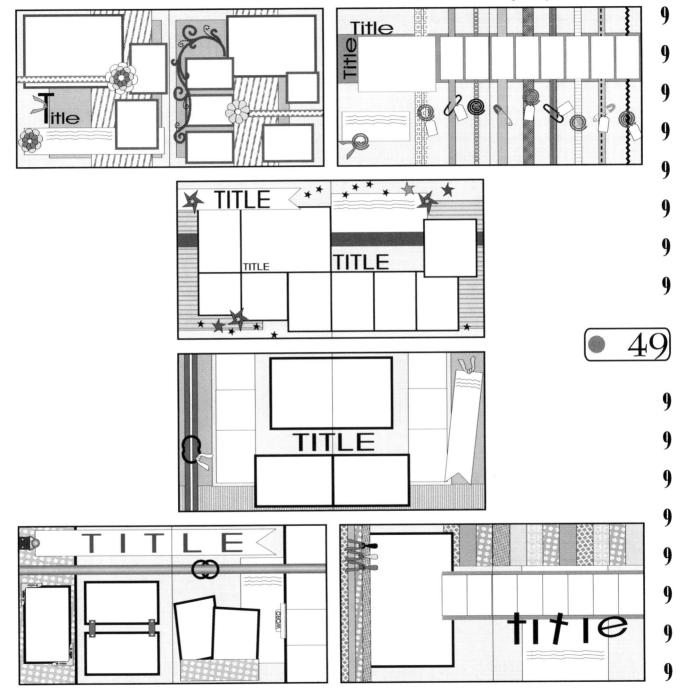

49

Double Page Layout Patterns

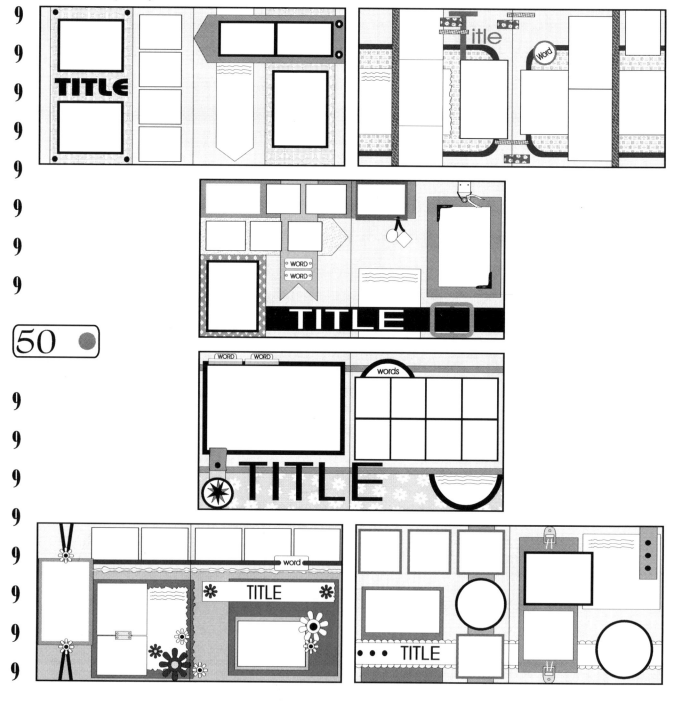

Double Page Layout Patterns

Double Page Layout Patterns

52

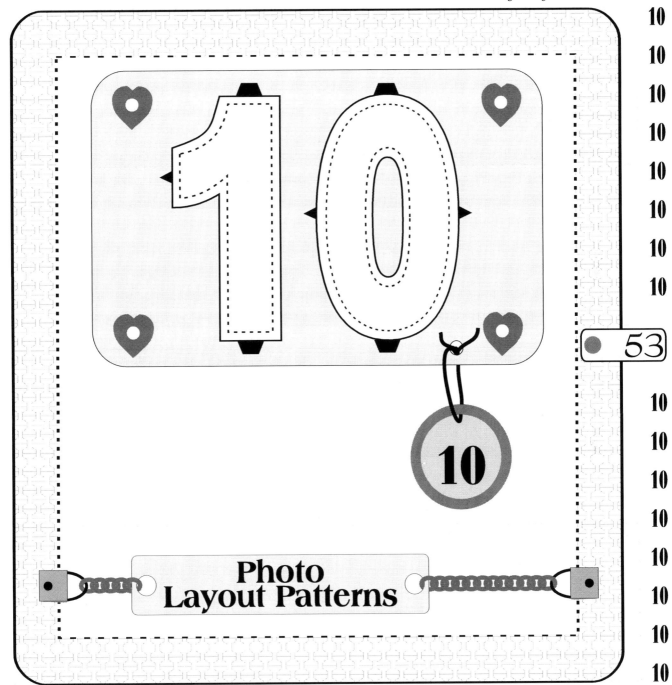

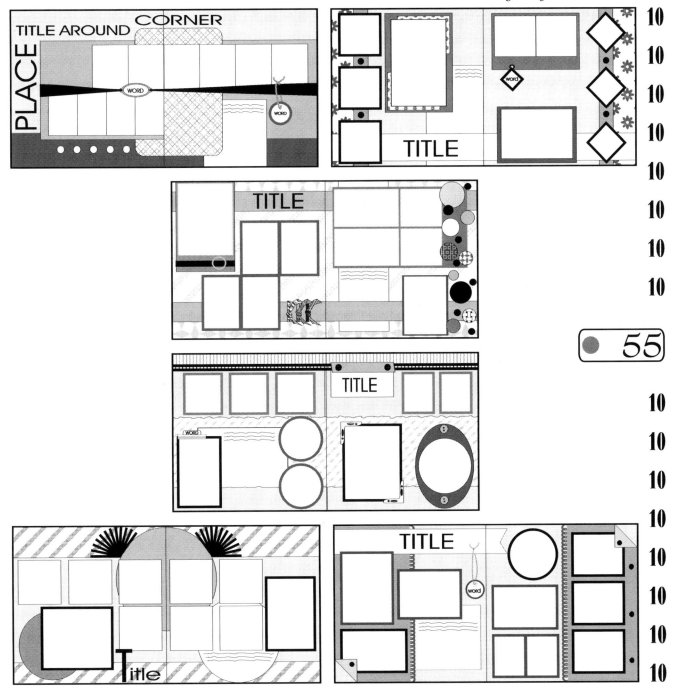

Double Page Layout Patterns

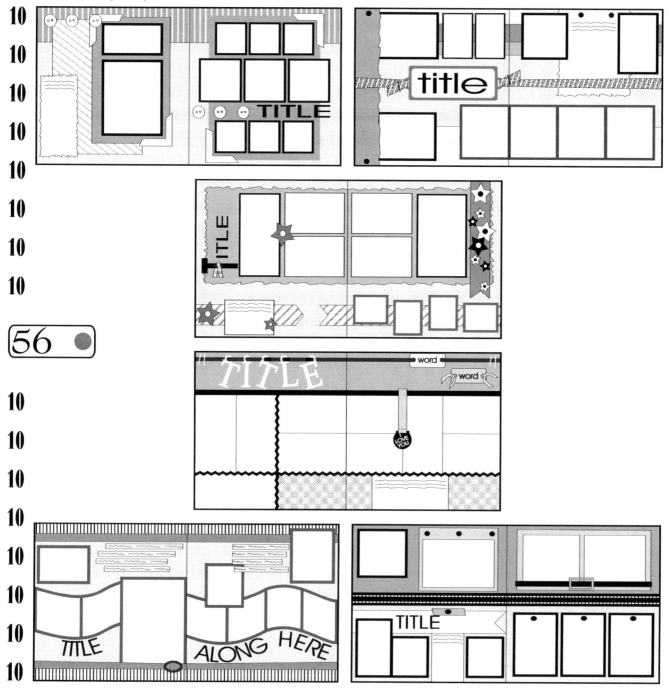

Double Page Layout Patterns

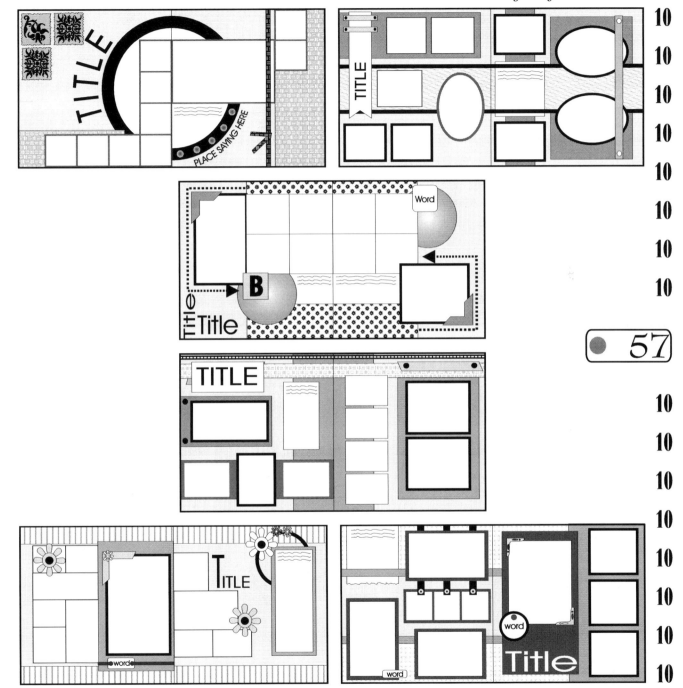

57

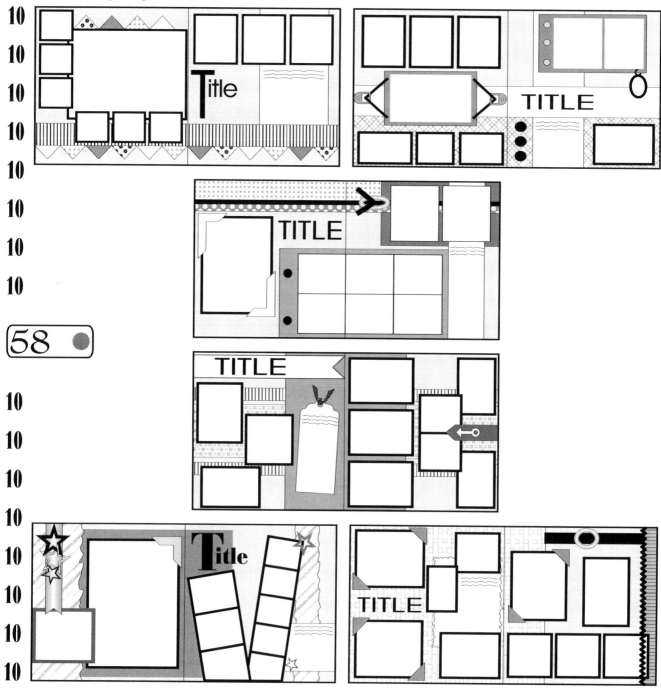

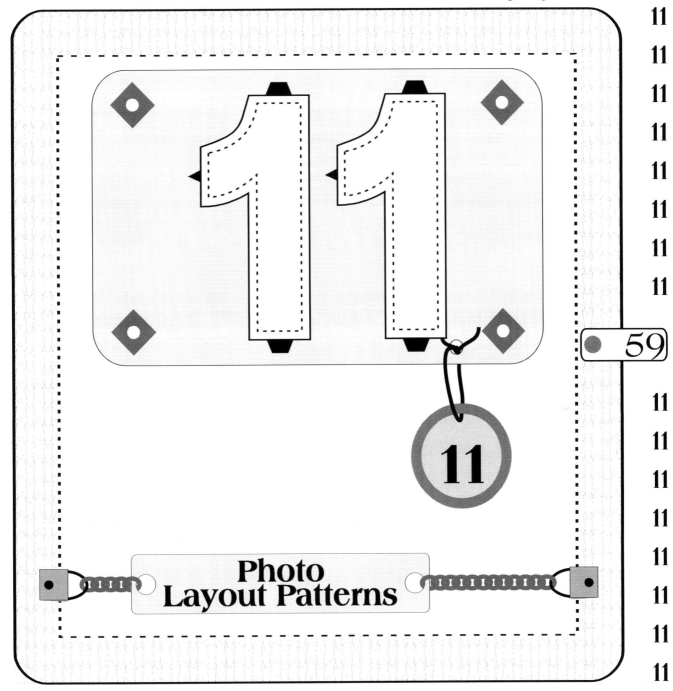

Double Page Layout Patterns

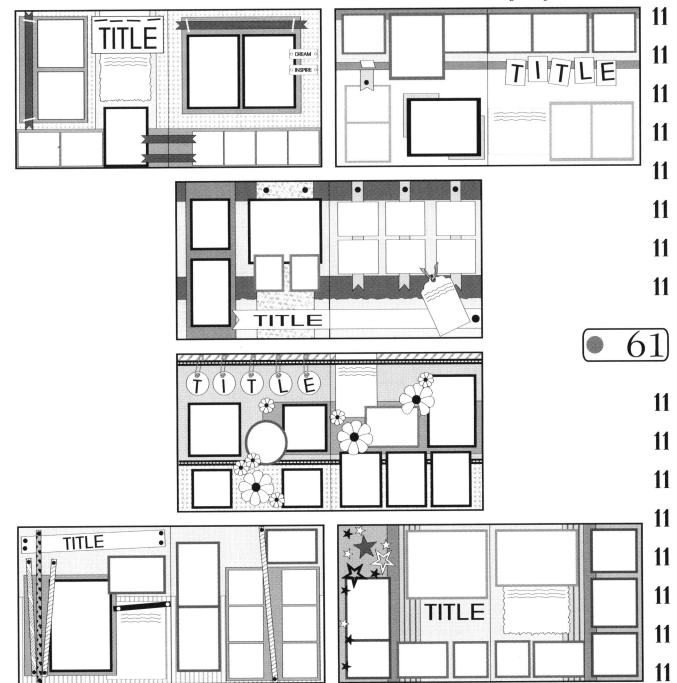

Double Page Layout Patterns

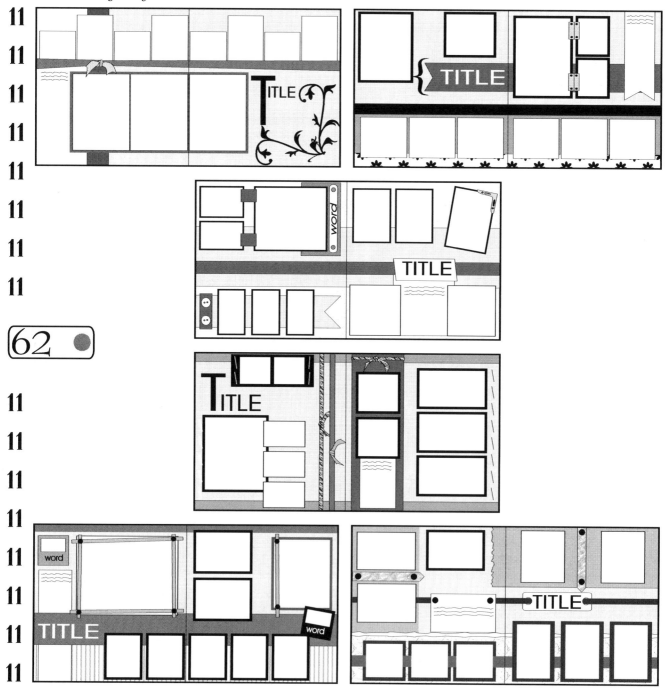

Double Page Layout Patterns

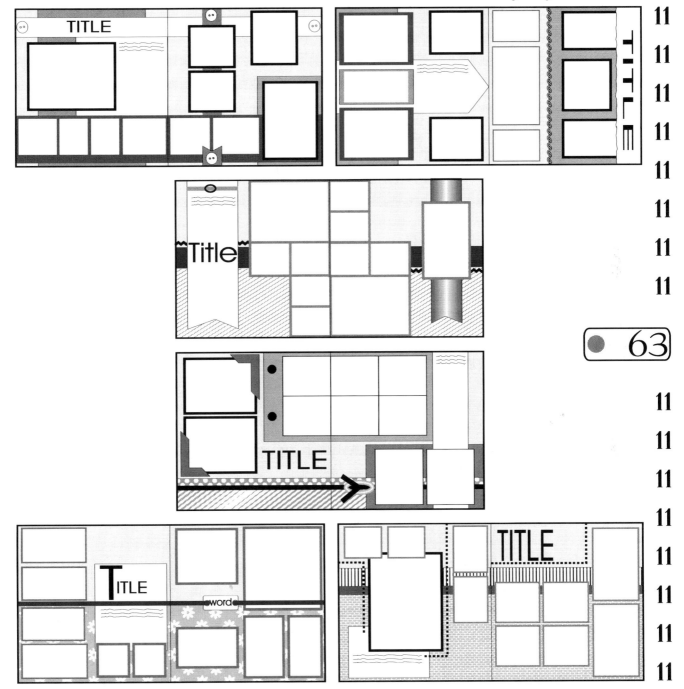

63

Double Page Layout Patterns

64

Double Page Layout Patterns

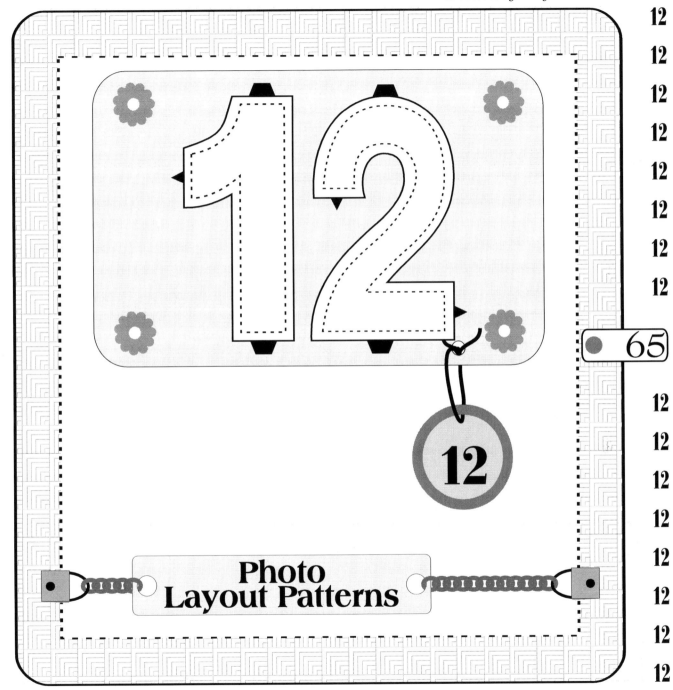

Photo Layout Patterns

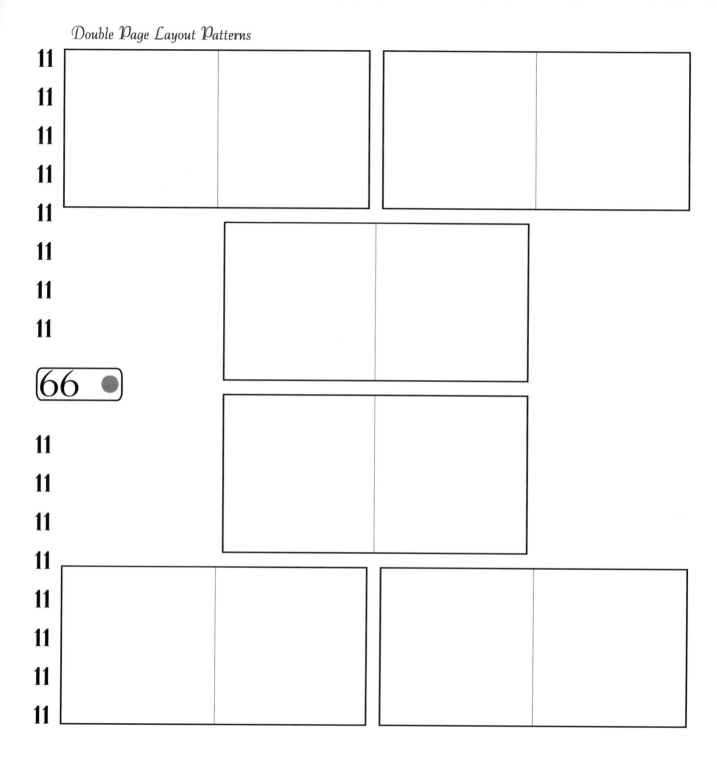

Double Page Layout Patterns

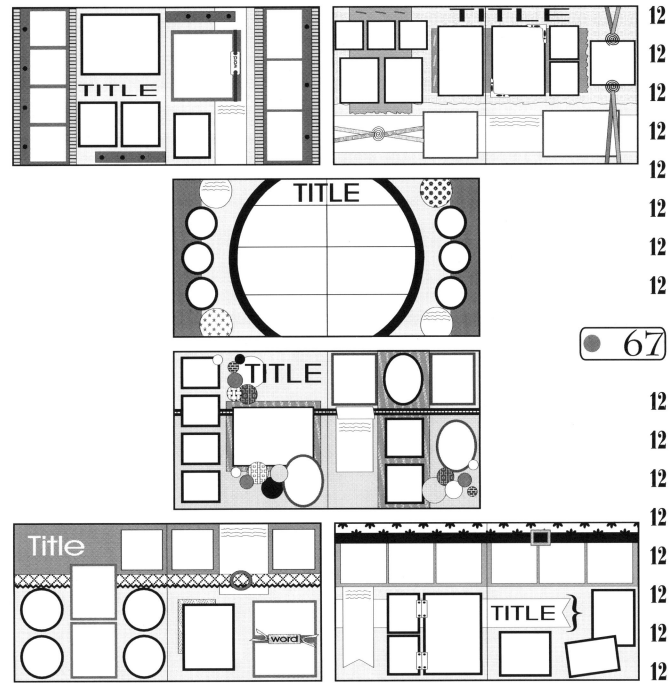

67

Double Page Layout Patterns

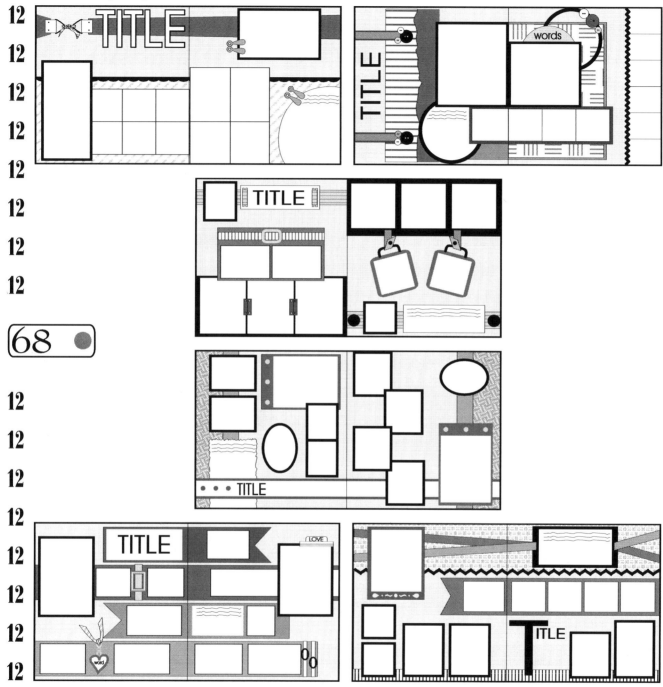

Double Page Layout Patterns

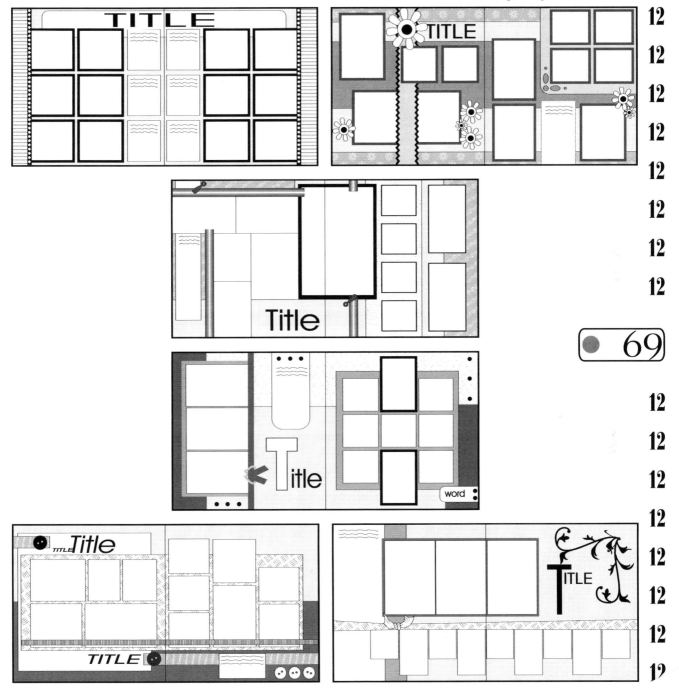

Double Page Layout Patterns

70

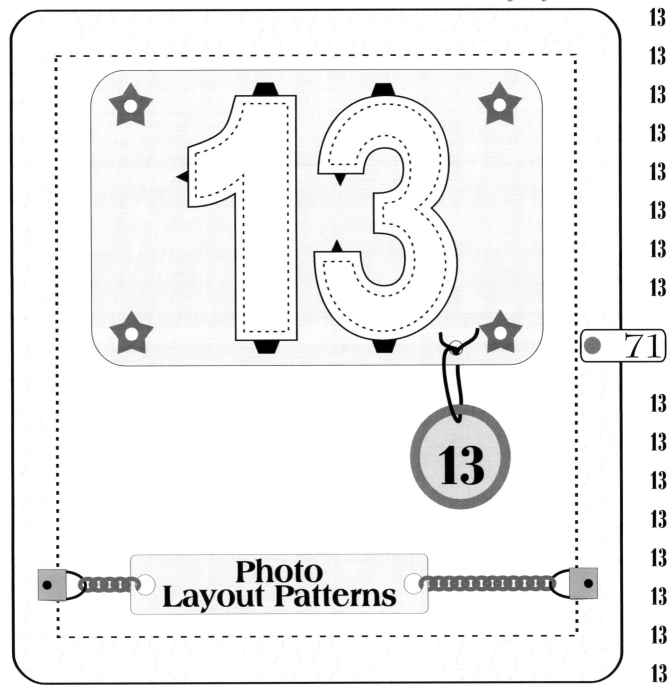

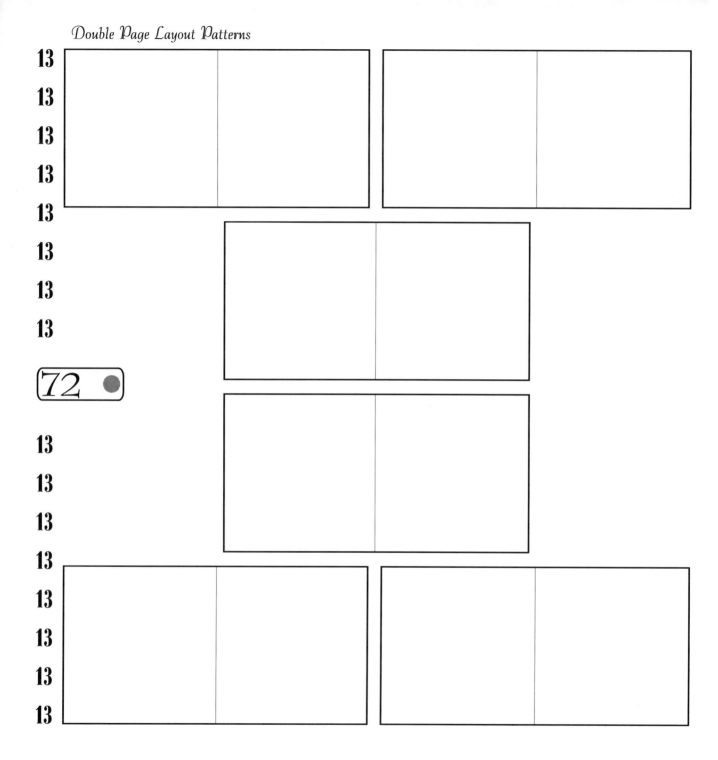

Double Page Layout Patterns

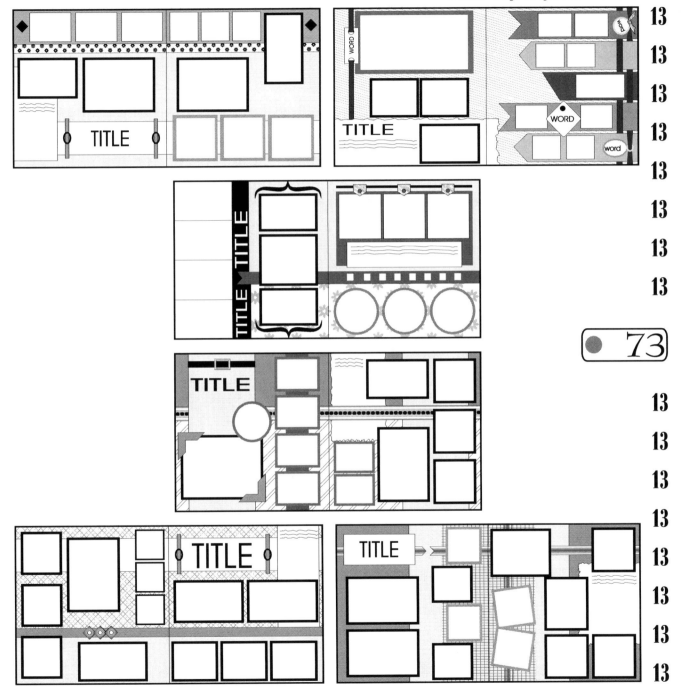

Double Page Layout Patterns

74

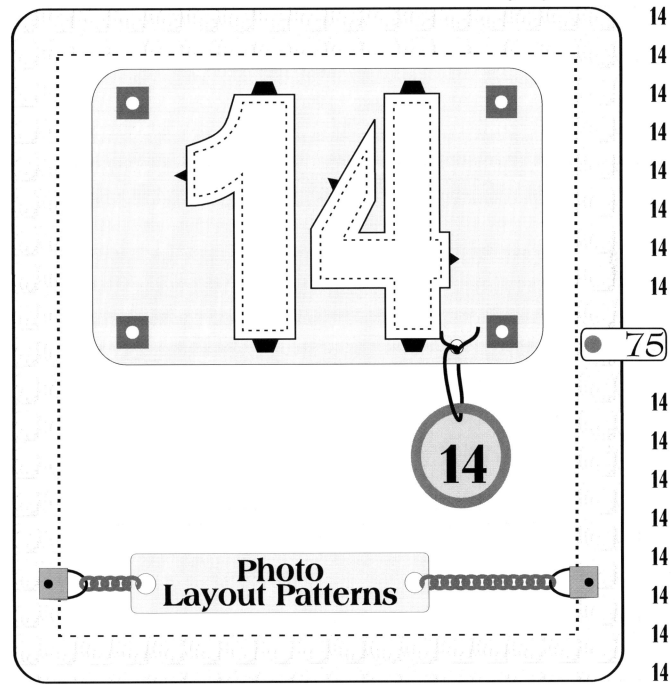

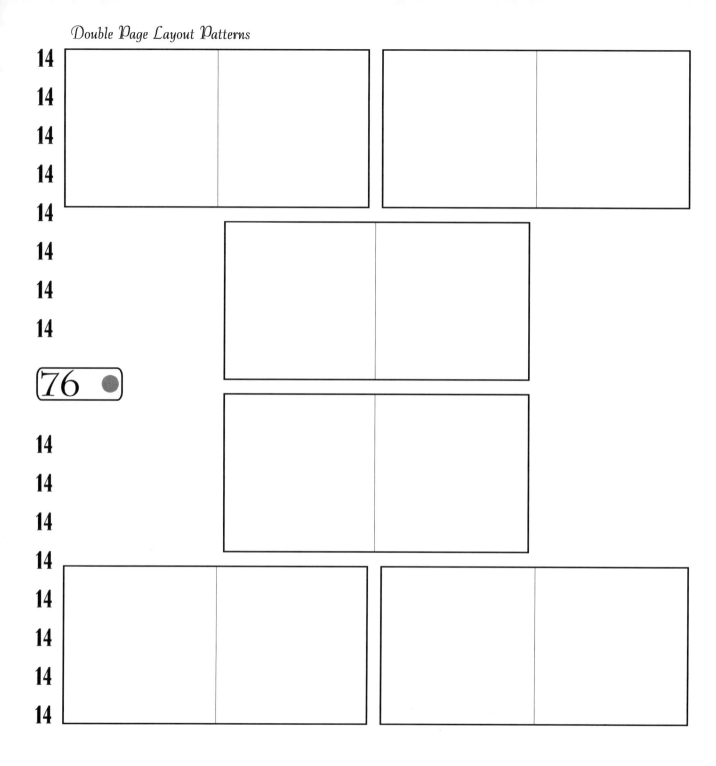

Double Page Layout Patterns

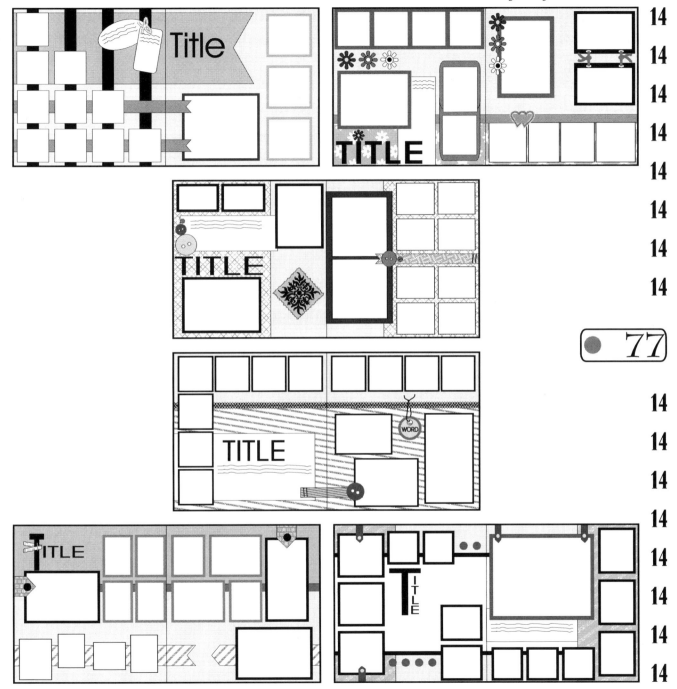

77

Double Page Layout Patterns

78

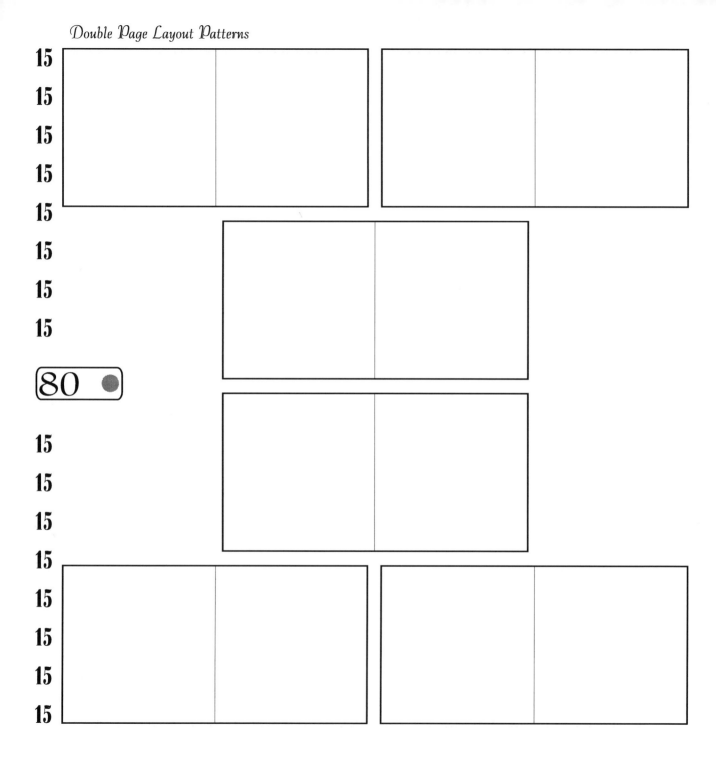

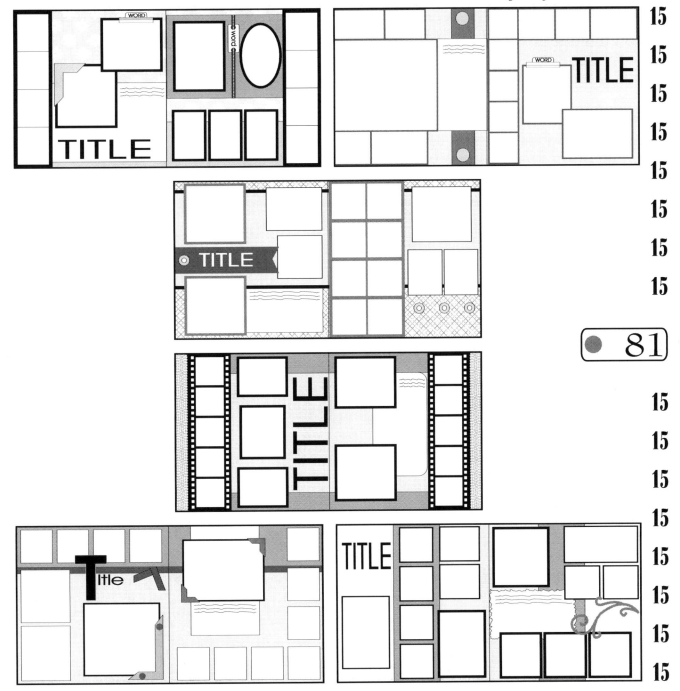

Double Page Layout Patterns

82

Double Page Layout Patterns

Double Page Layout Patterns

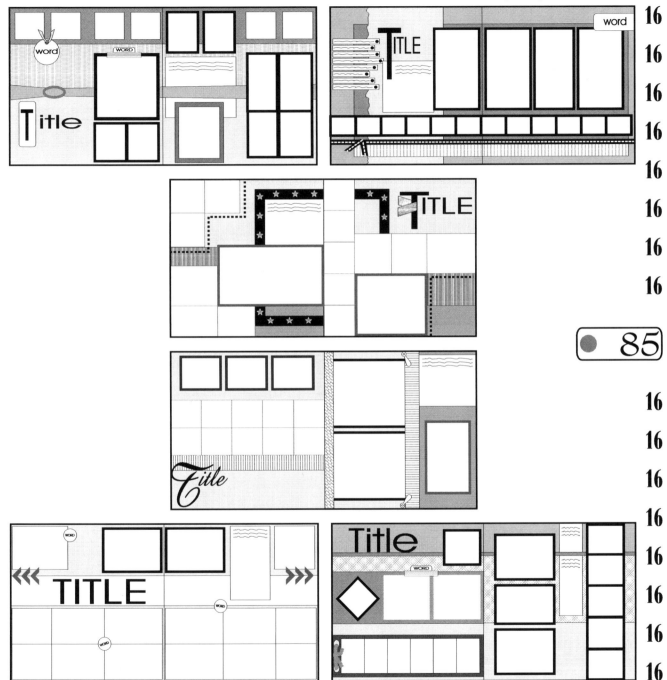

85

Double Page Layout Patterns

86

Double Page Layout Patterns

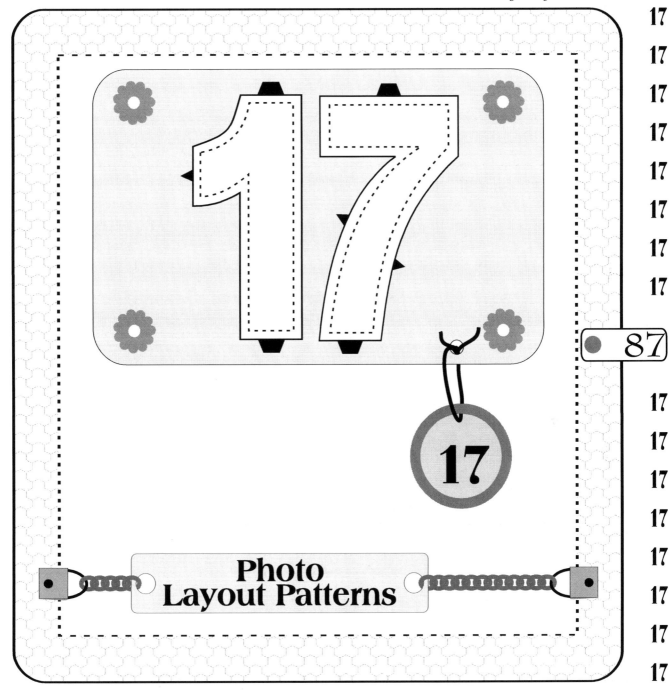

87

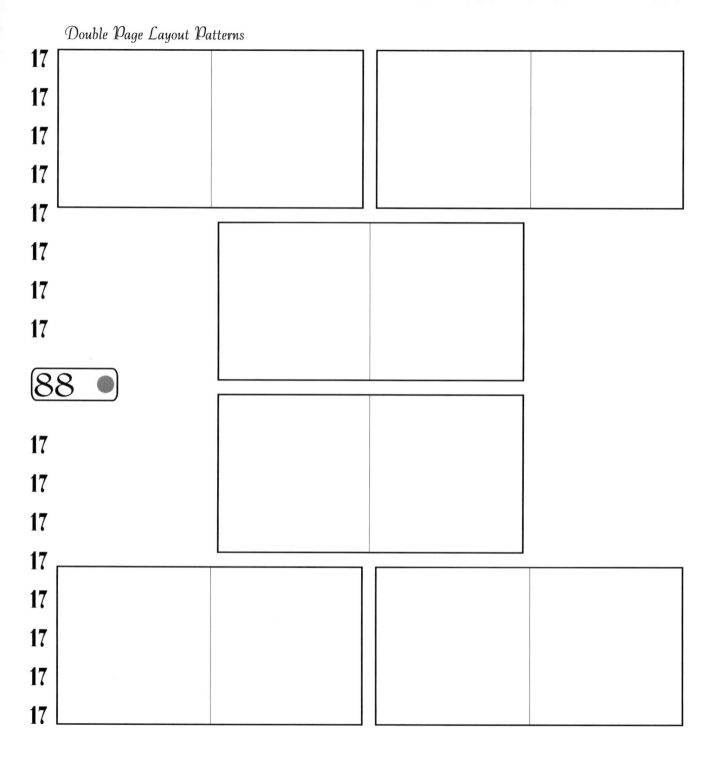

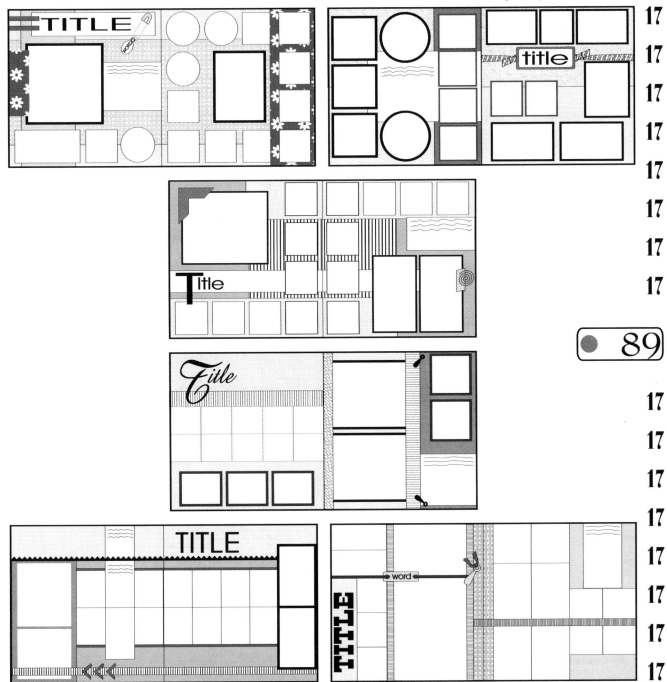

Double Page Layout Patterns

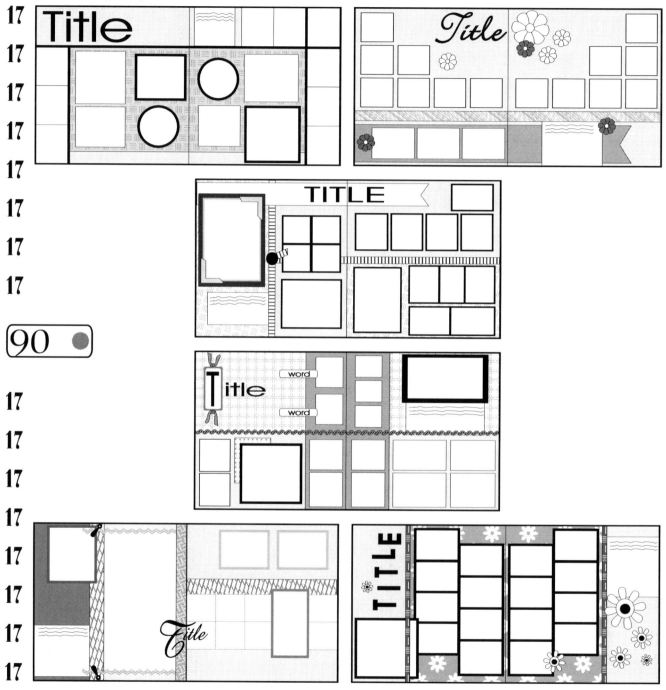

90

Double Page Layout Patterns

18 & 19

Photo Layout Patterns

91

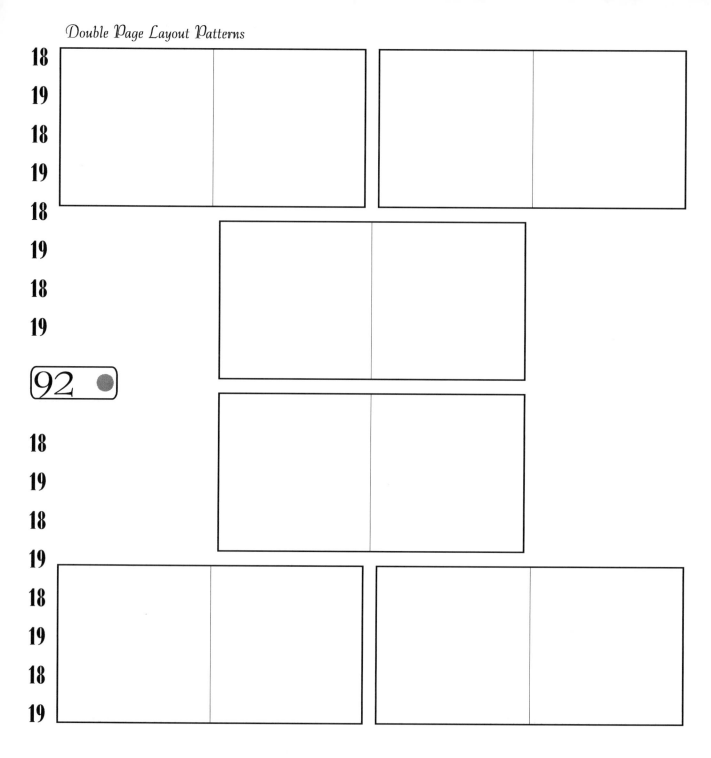

Double Page Layout Patterns

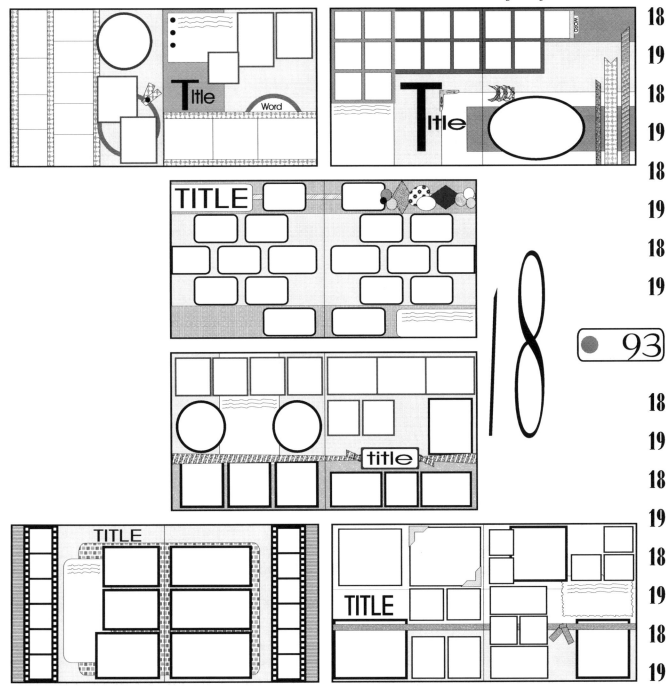

Double Page Layout Patterns

94

Double Page Layout Patterns

95

Double Page Layout Patterns

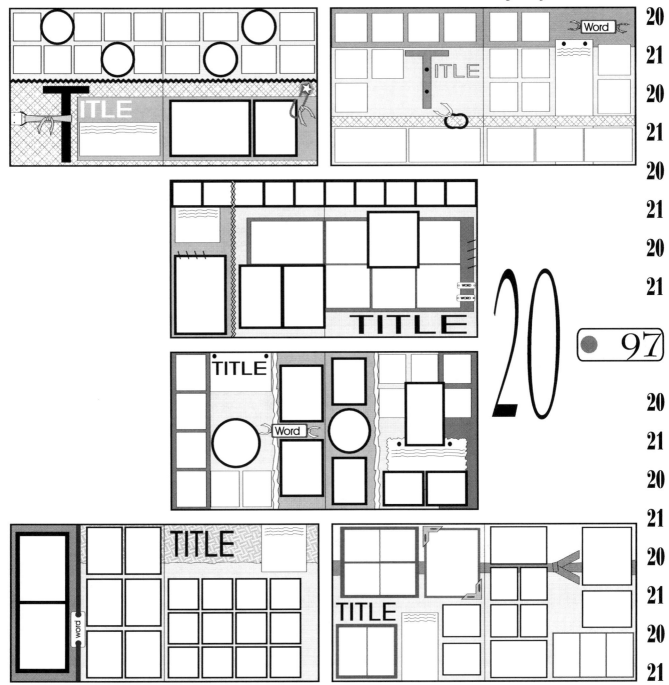

Double Page Layout Patterns

98

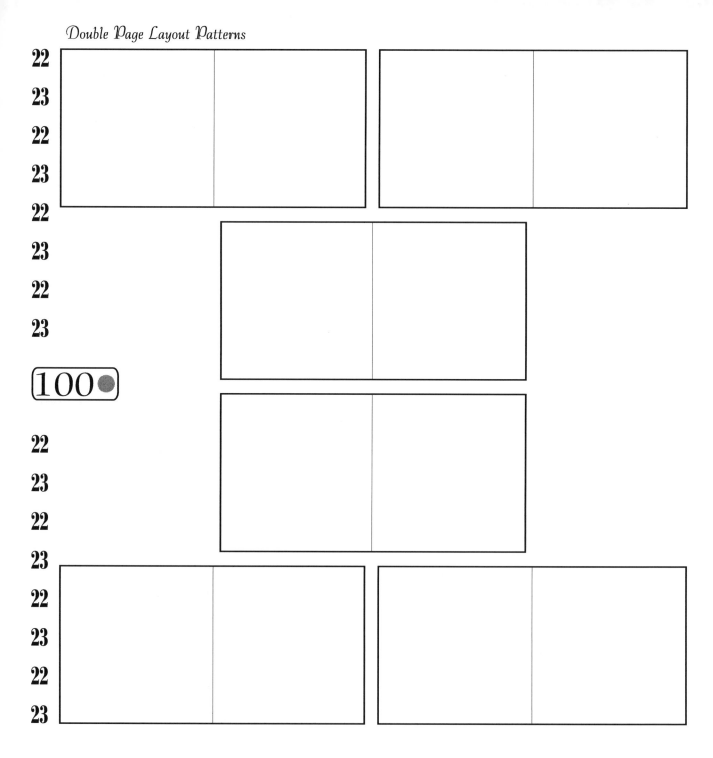

Double Page Layout Patterns

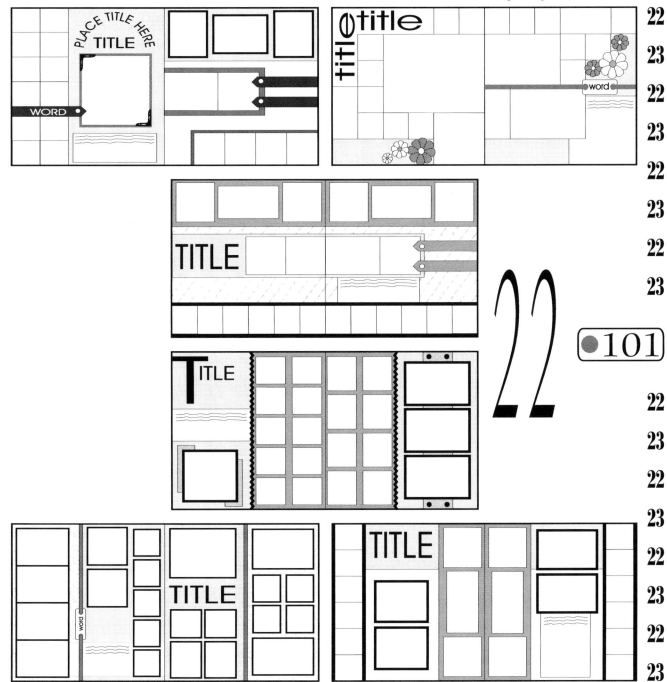

Double Page Layout Patterns

102

Double Page Layout Patterns

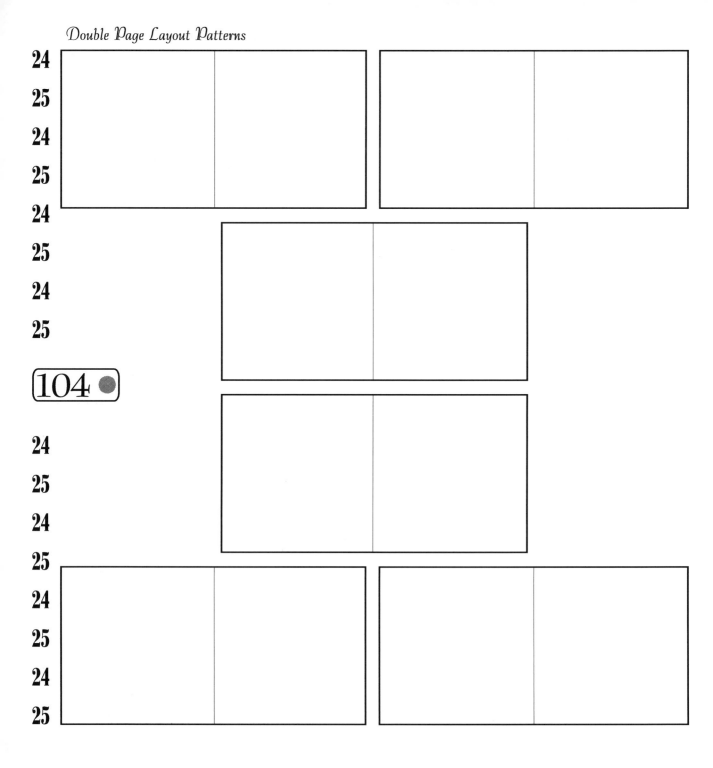

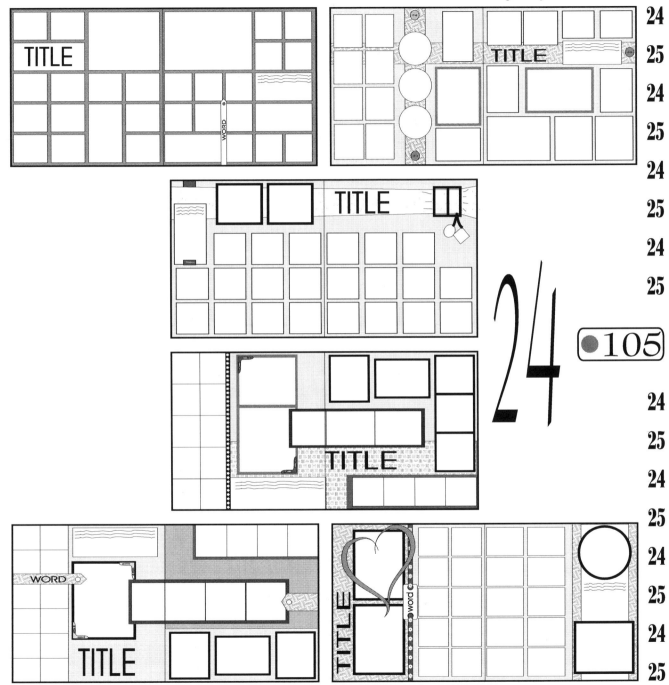

Double Page Layout Patterns

106　25

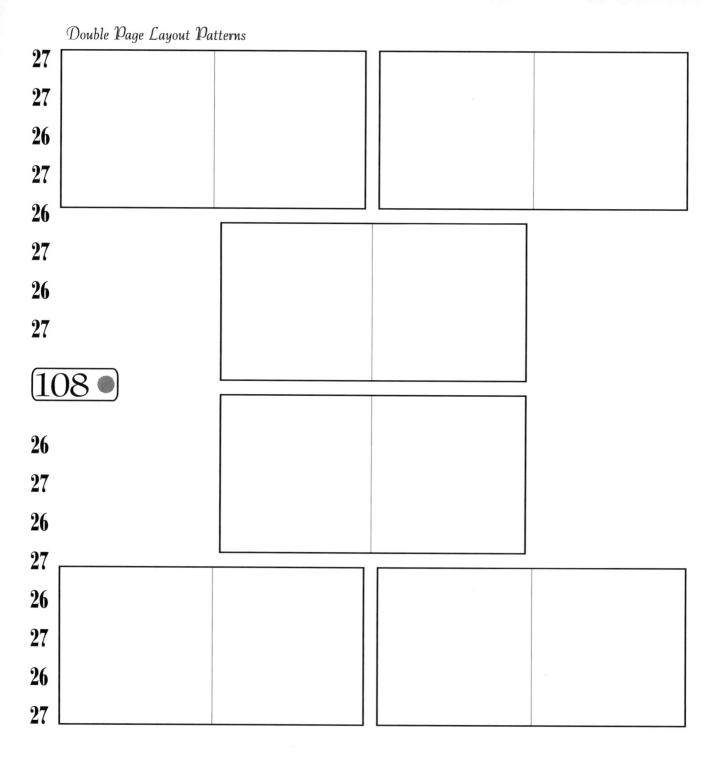

Double Page Layout Patterns

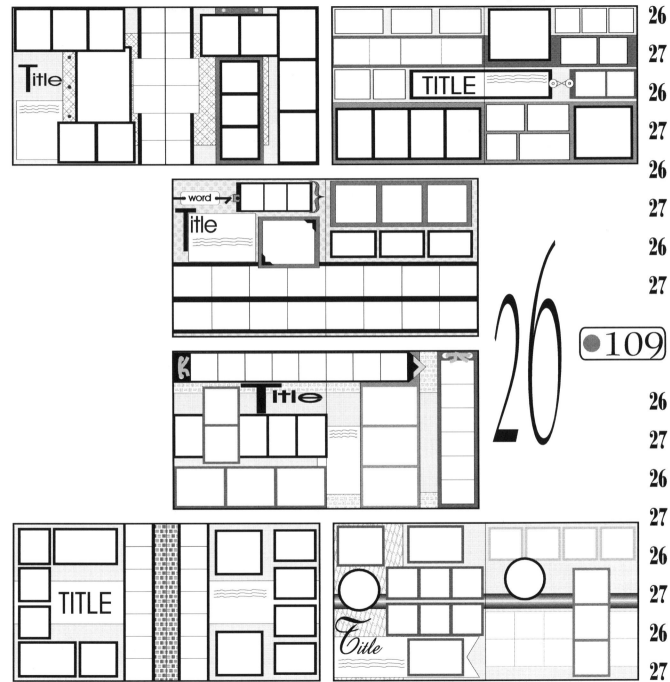

Double Page Layout Patterns

Double Page Layout Patterns

Double Page Layout Patterns

114

Double Page Layout Patterns

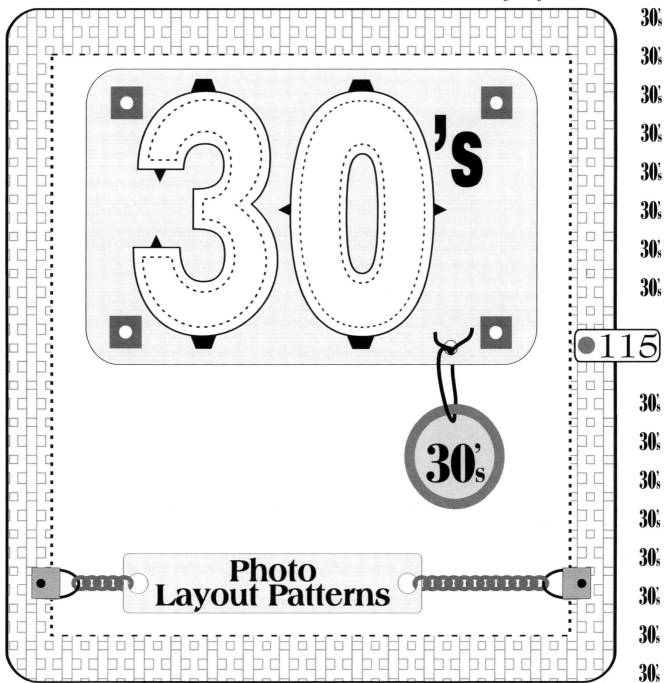

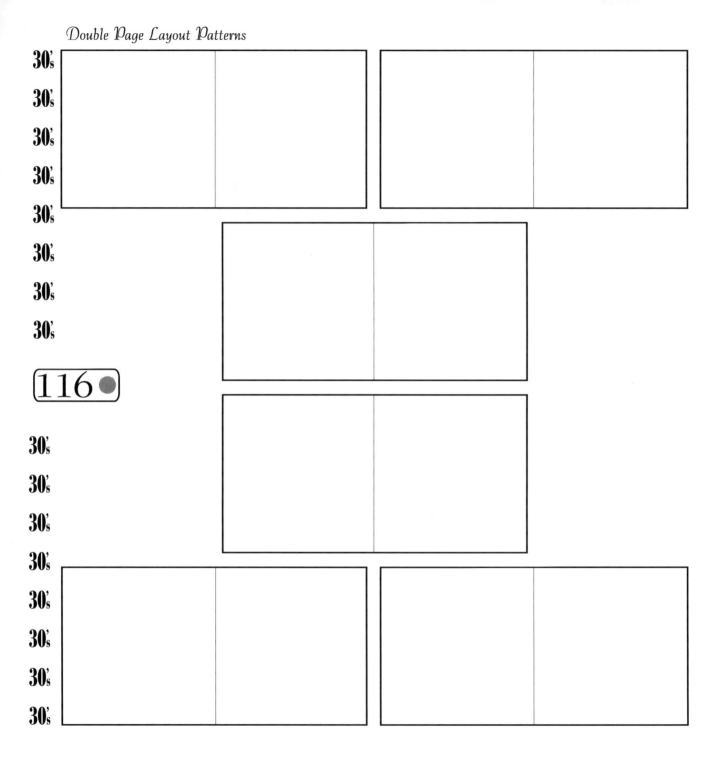

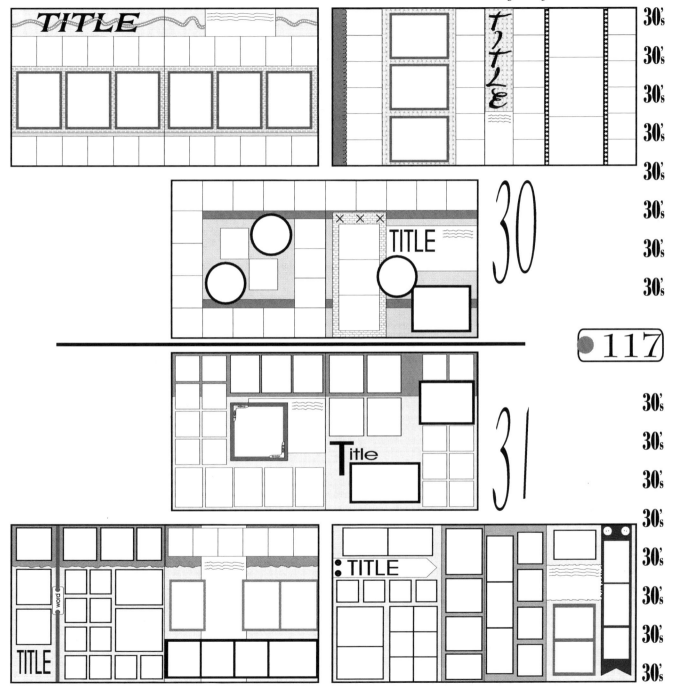

Double Page Layout Patterns

32

33

118

Double Page Layout Patterns

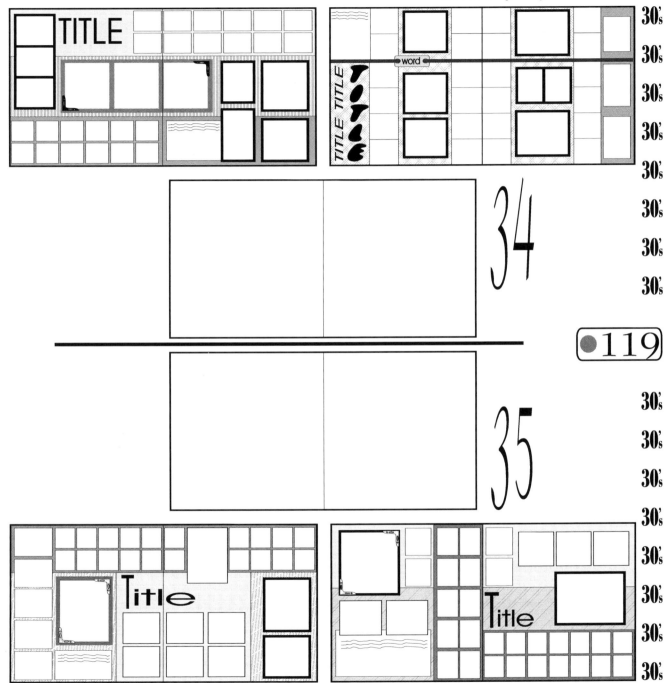

Double Page Layout Patterns

Single Page Layout Patterns

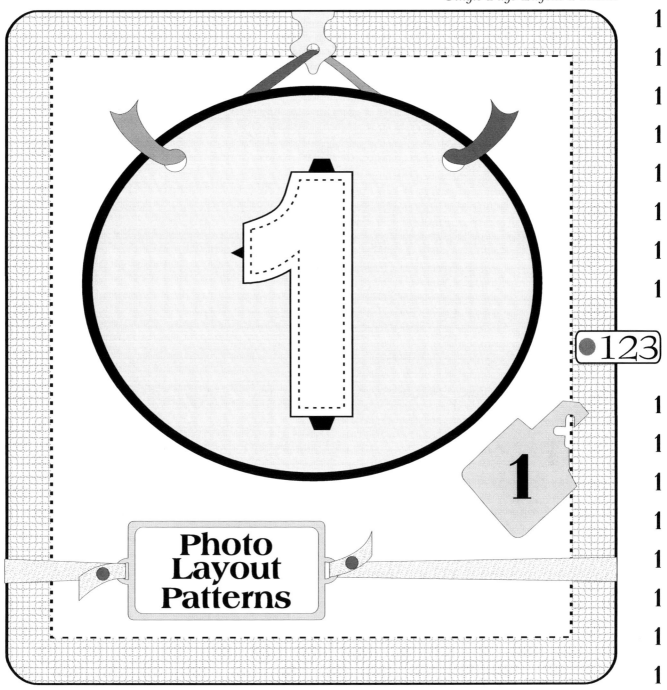

Single Page Layout Patterns

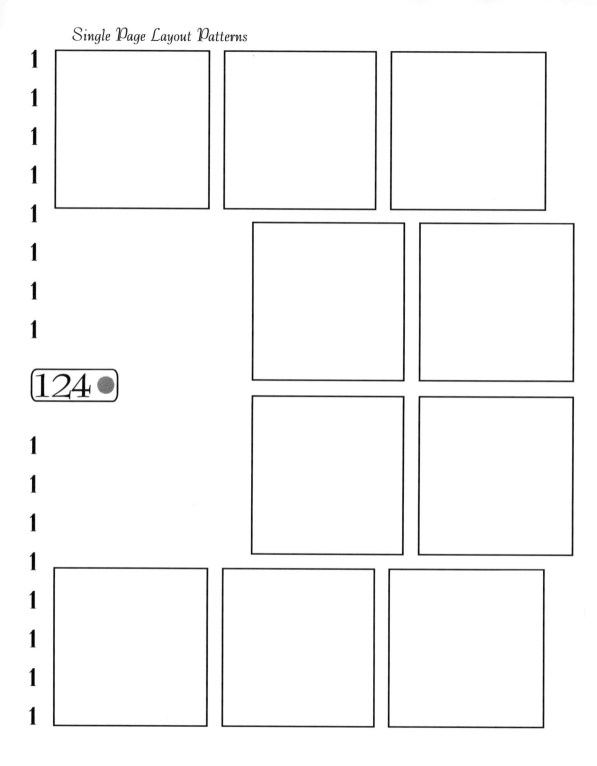

124

Single Page Layout Patterns

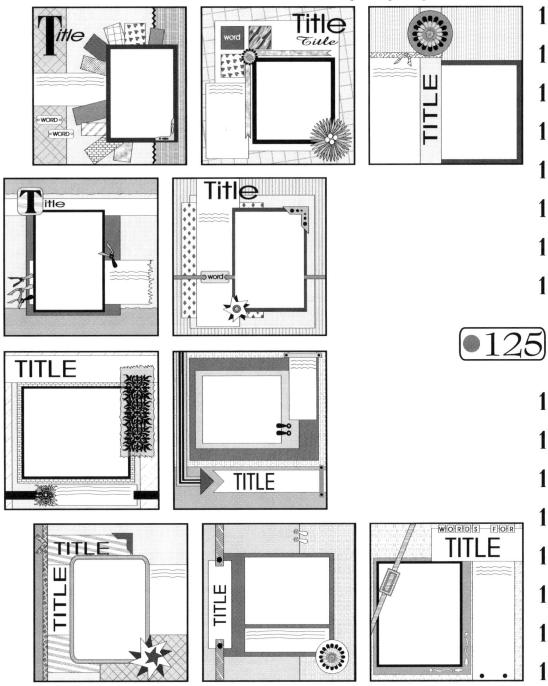

Single Page Layout Patterns

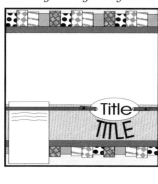

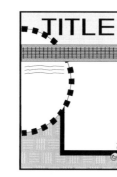
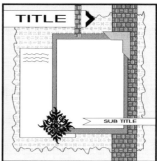
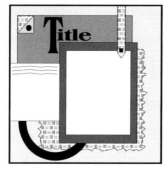

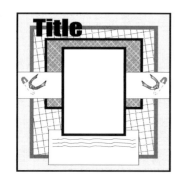

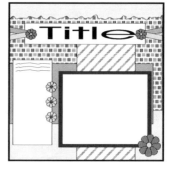

126

Single Page Layout Patterns

2

Photo Layout Patterns

•127

Single Page Layout Patterns

128

Single Page Layout Patterns

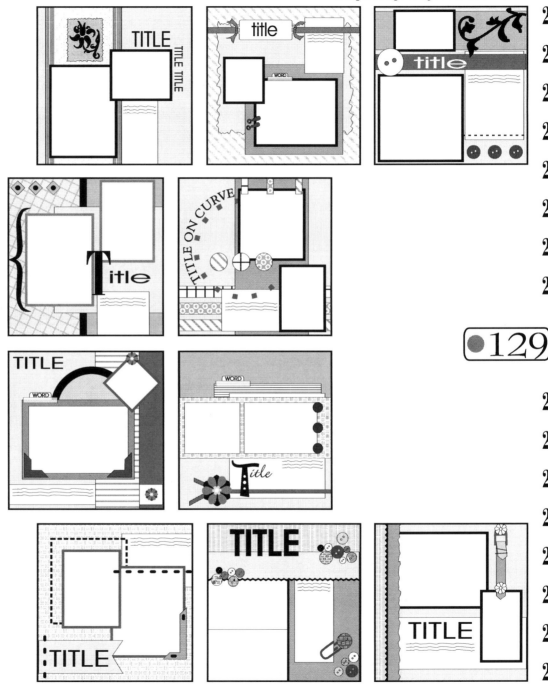

129

Single Page Layout Patterns

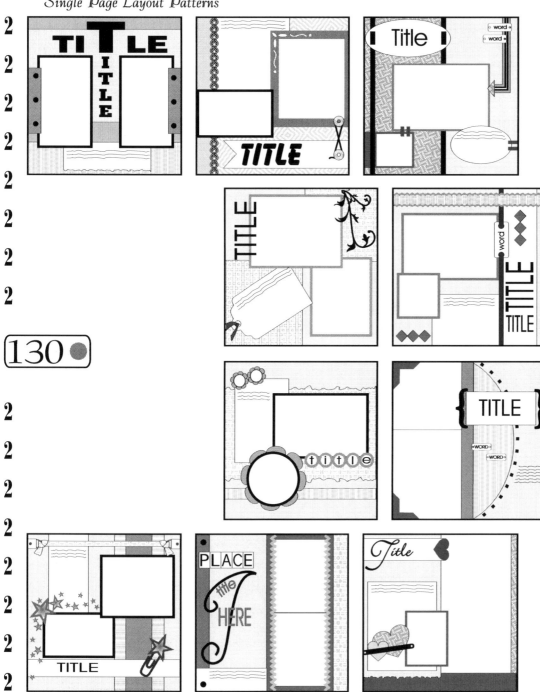

130

Single Page Layout Patterns

3

Photo Layout Patterns

Single Page Layout Patterns

132

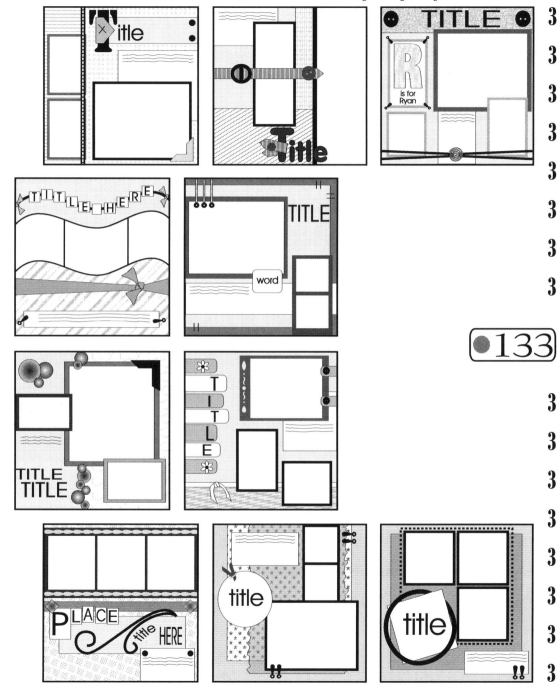

Single Page Layout Patterns

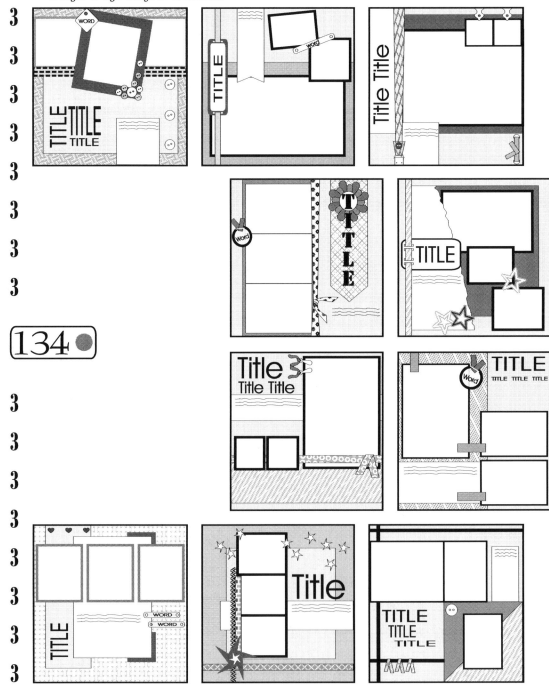

134

Single Page Layout Patterns

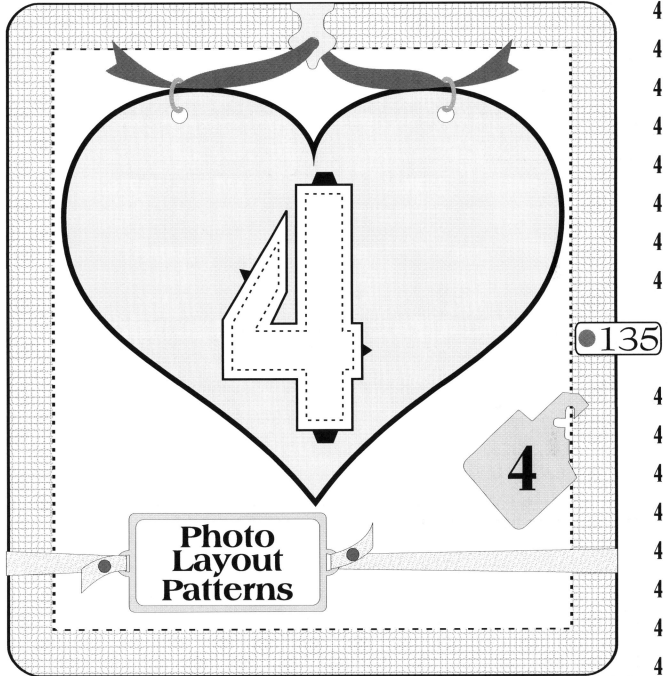

Single Page Layout Patterns

Single Page Layout Patterns

137

Single Page Layout Patterns

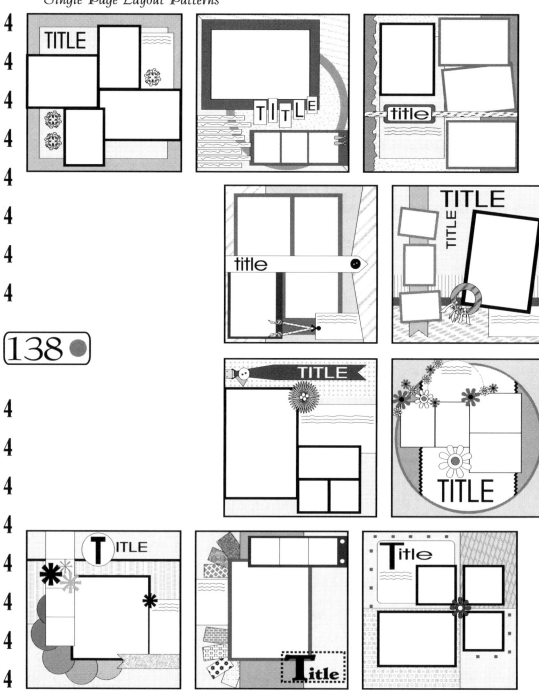

138

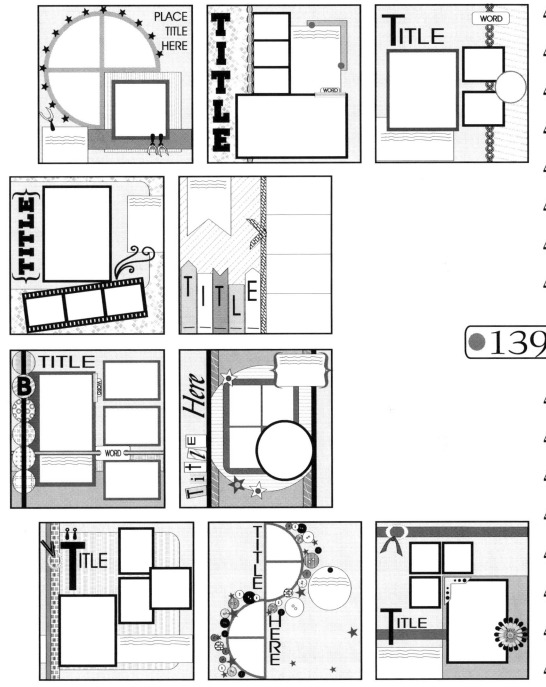

Single Page Layout Patterns

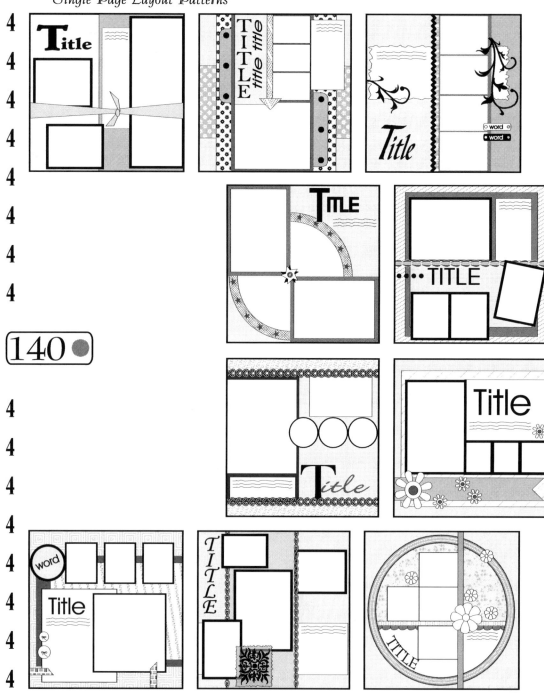

140

Single Page Layout Patterns

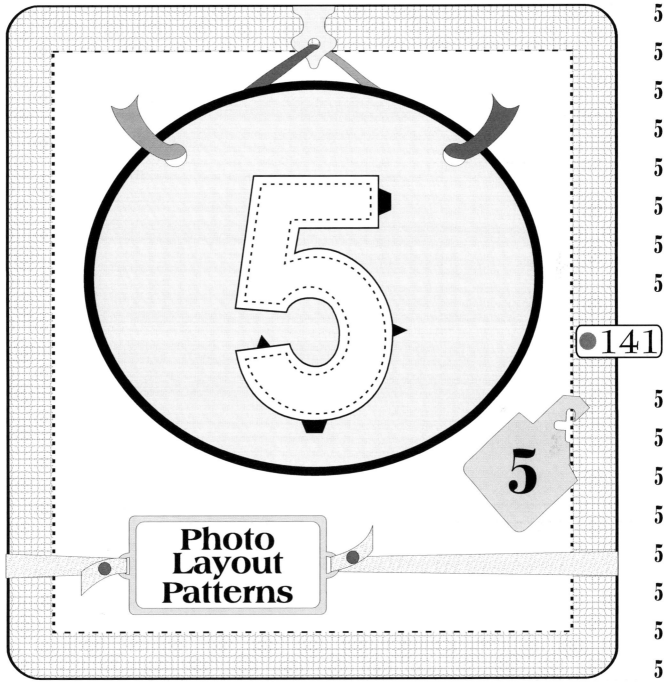

Single Page Layout Patterns

142

Single Page Layout Patterns

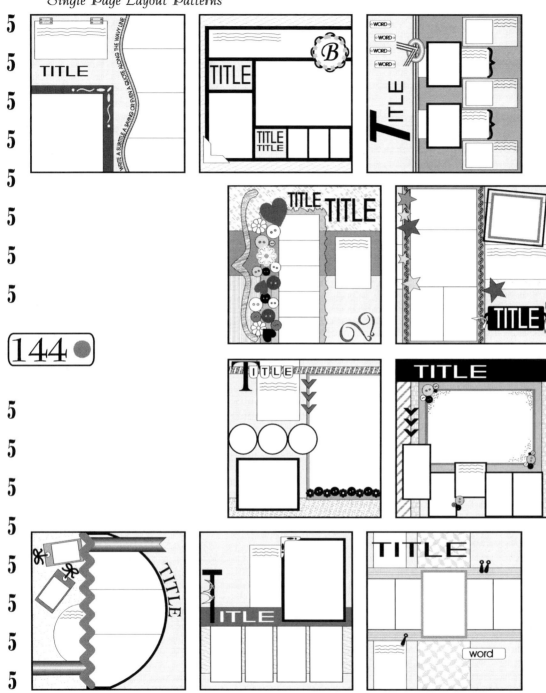

Single Page Layout Patterns

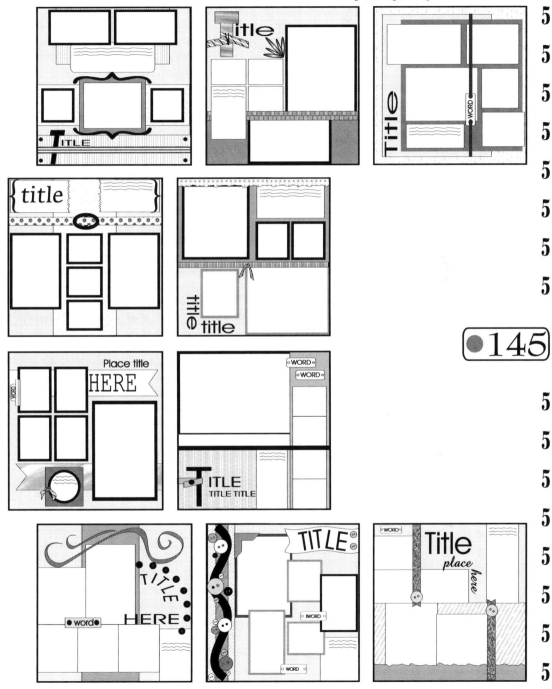

145

Single Page Layout Patterns

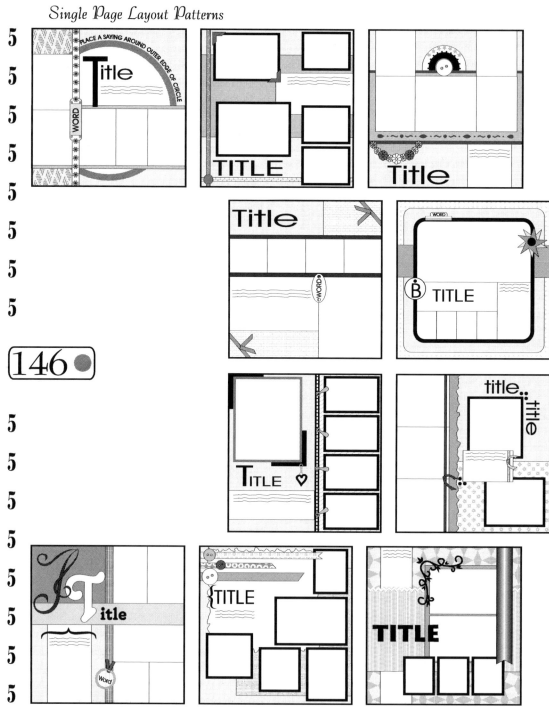

146

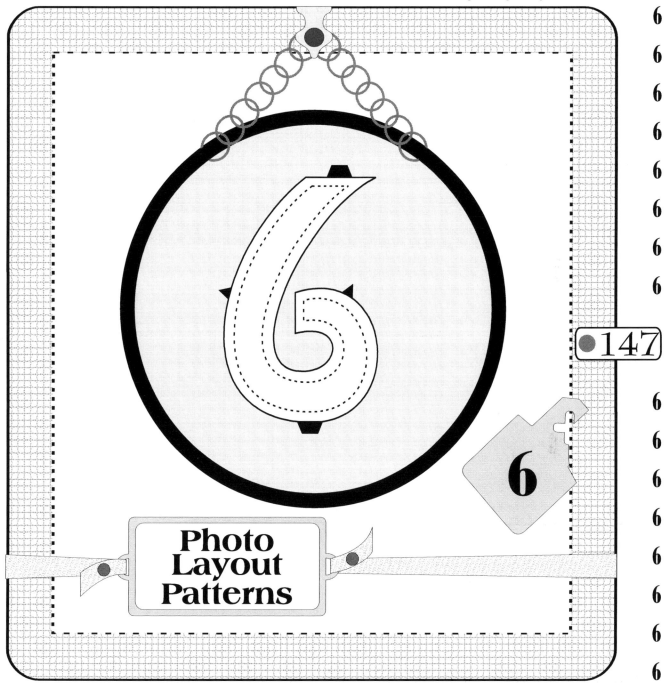

Single Page Layout Patterns

148

Single Page Layout Patterns

149

Single Page Layout Patterns

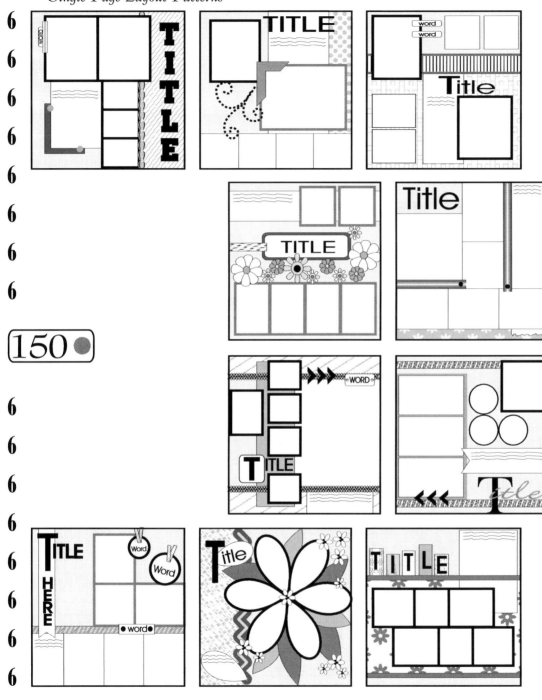

150

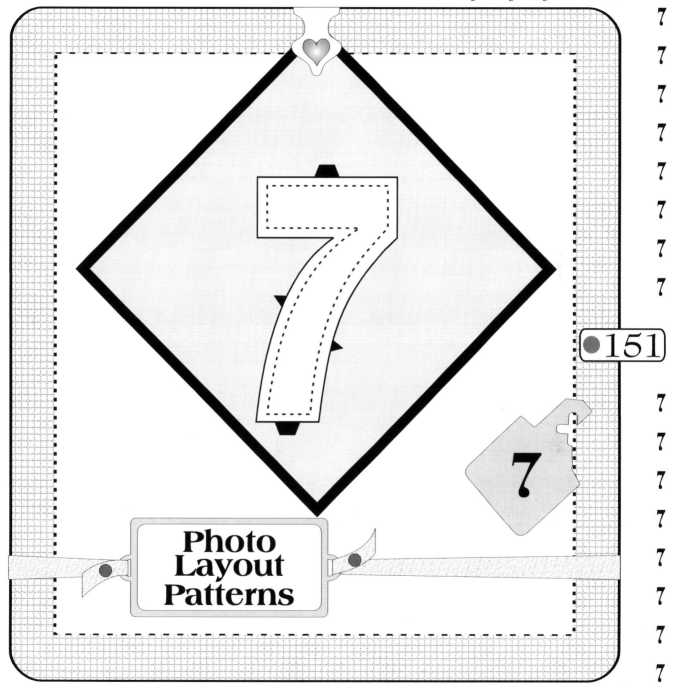

Single Page Layout Patterns

7 • 151

Photo Layout Patterns

Single Page Layout Patterns

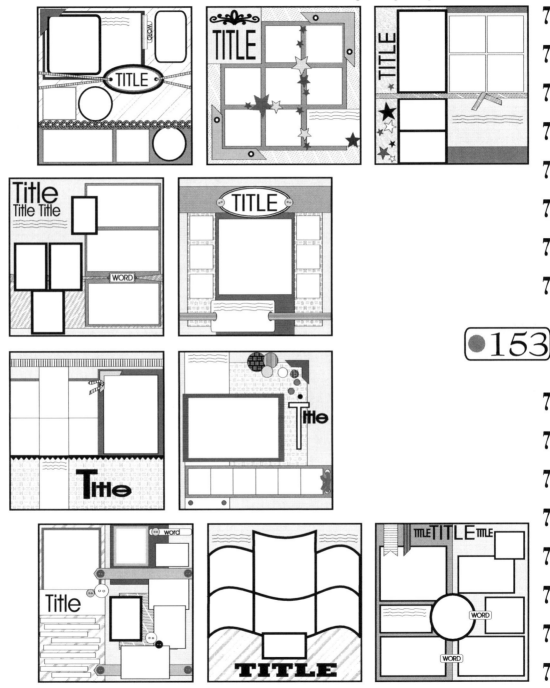

153

Single Page Layout Patterns

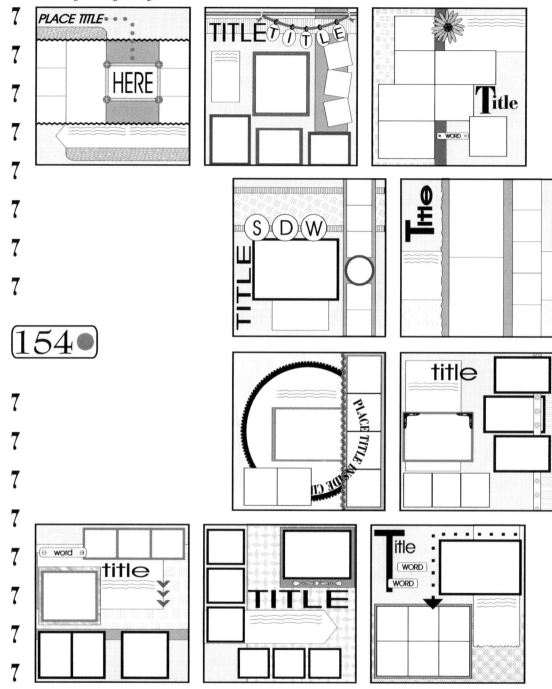

154

Single Page Layout Patterns

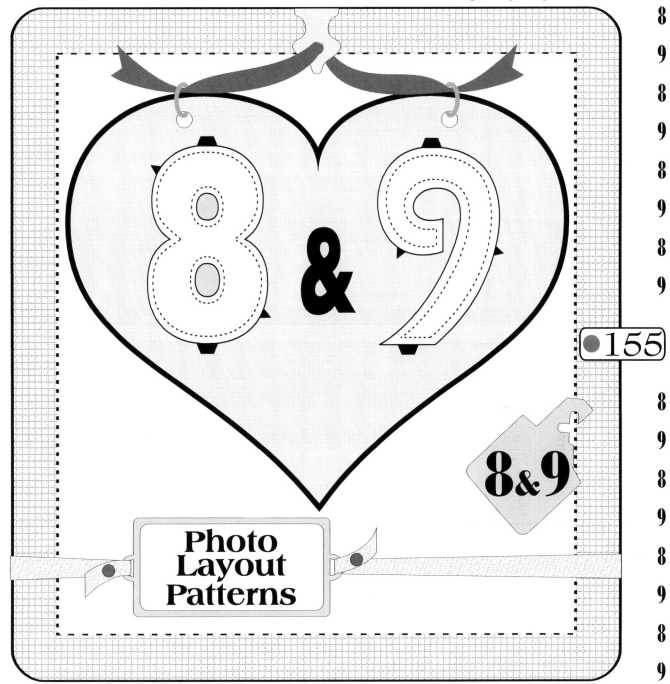

Single Page Layout Patterns

156

Single Page Layout Patterns

157

Single Page Layout Patterns

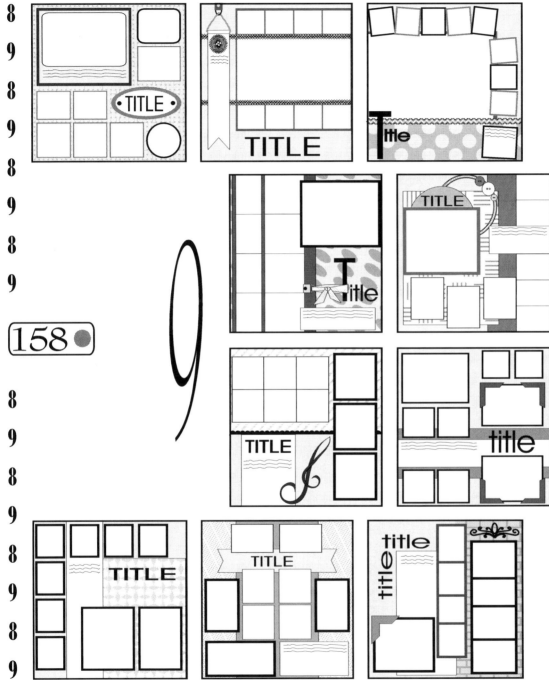

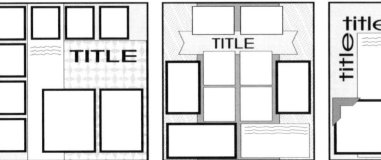

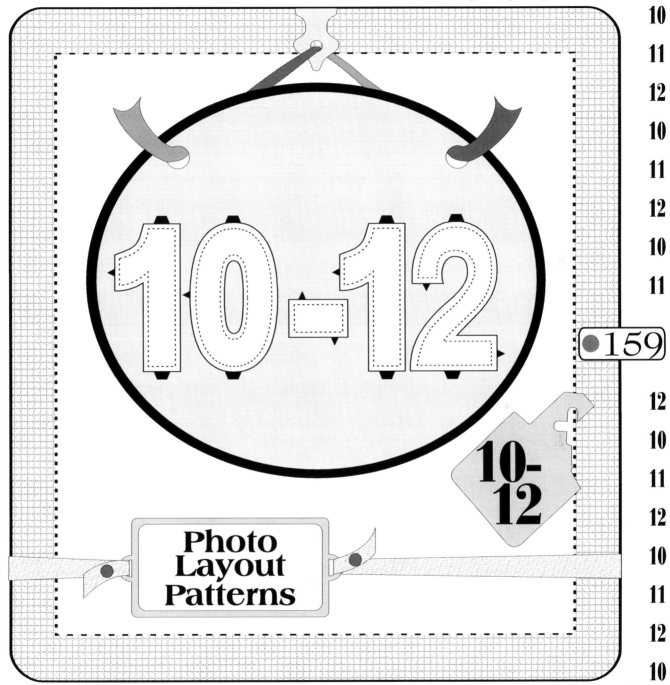

Single Page Layout Patterns

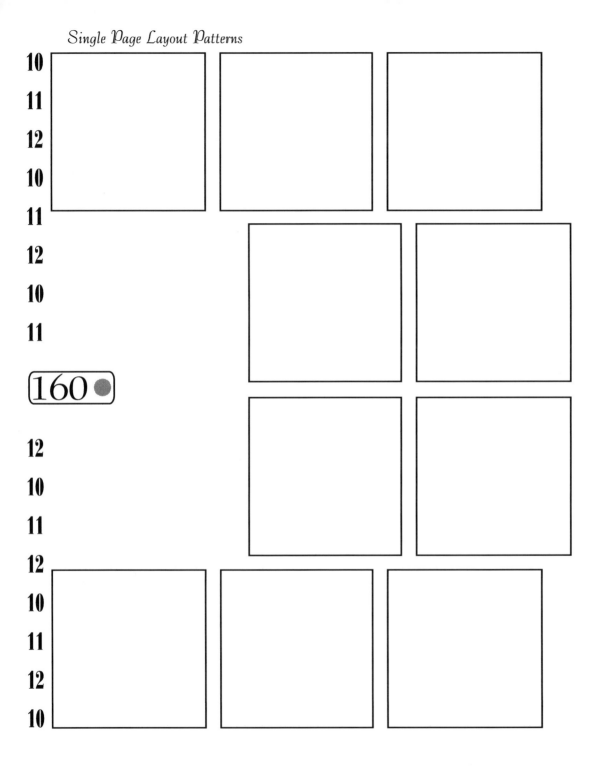

160

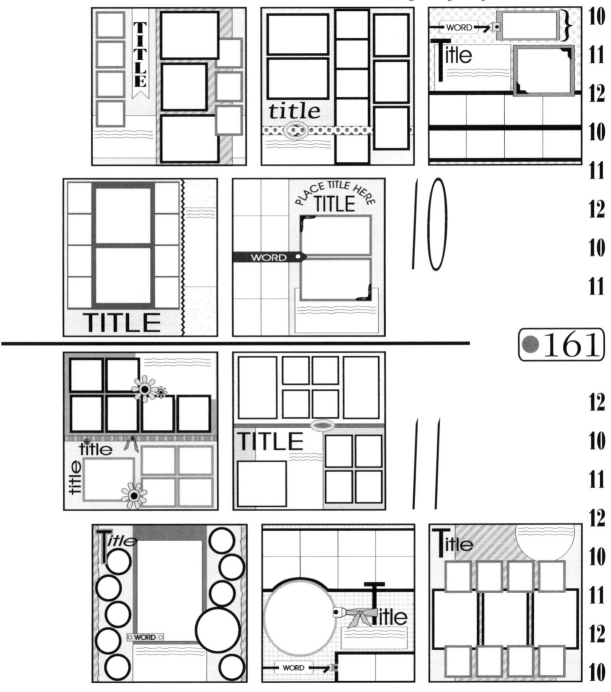

Single Page Layout Patterns

162

Patterns Size Conversion Charts

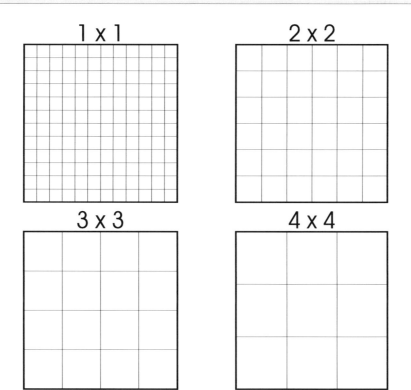

Use these conversion charts in helping to size your photos to fit the pattern your using. When fully sized, these charts and single Page Patterns are 12 x 12 and double Page Patterns are 12 x 24. Easily get correct measurements for your photos or mattings by matching your selected pattern against the conversion chart sizes.

Copy this page on to a Transparency for easier use with the Page Patterns.

Page Patterns

Made in the USA
Middletown, DE
18 June 2017